# CLEAR
# FOR
# TAKE-OFF
## and hope
## for the best!

# CLEAR
# FOR
# TAKE-OFF
## and hope
## for the best!

*Don't worry, nothing
in this book will
scare you!*

*JmC*

## John Campbell

*This book is dedicated to*
*Geoff Large, Watch Supervisor,*
*Mentor and Friend*

Heathrow Airport ATC

1977 - 1981

# Contents

# Acknowledgements

The author would like to thank:

Derek Neley for the SH360, TWA 747, GBRYA, and the Manchester Mozzy photographs and for his kind permission to include them in this book.

Mel Whapshare for the diagram of "Shooting the Gap" and for a first reading of the manuscript as an aviation expert.

His partner Sonya for a first reading of the manuscript as a non-aviation expert.

My partner Geraldine for putting up with the frustrations emanating from my office during the writing of the manuscript as well as the time it took to do so.

Covid19 for providing the lockdown in 2021 when this book was written.

Pat McGleenon, a fellow controller at Belfast International Airport for giving me the inspiration for the title.

Robert Mason, author of the book Chickenhawk, for his excellent tales of helicopter flying in Vietnam, inspiring me to write this book.

Kristoffer and the excellent team at Publishing Push without whom this book would never have been printed.

Sir Billy Connolly for his book Tall Tales and Wee Stories which not only inspired the title of a chapter but also the hope that beigeness has been removed from British aviation.

And finally, to all ATC staff, flight deck crew and cabin crew whom I have met around the world, my sincere thanks for allowing me to infest your "office" and for happily answering my interminable questions!

# Preface

Aviation is a hard-nosed industry in the sense that if you make a mistake that you don't fix immediately, it will deal with you severely! So many accidents are the end result of a long string of faults and mistakes. If only one of those mistakes had been corrected, the accident would never have happened.

All aviation operational staff work extremely hard. The concentration needed to position aircraft with hundreds of people on board onto the final approach of a busy airport or get them airborne and away safely is considerable. The attention to detail in flying an airliner requires an extensive understanding of the machine's systems. The determination required to guarantee a safe operation takes a massive commitment from all operational personnel. Combined, we have now created a safe and efficient mode of travel, although the pressures on aircrew and Air Traffic Control can be keenly felt. There has to be a safety valve, and humour supplies the perfect antidote to pressure. You might find the humour in this book a bit over the top, a bit risqué, a bit offensive. I don't apologise for that – it's the reader who will find any of the humour offensive. My colleagues and I found it invaluable.

I hope you have a good time reading this little collection of mine. I'd appreciate any comments and am always keen to hear about your own aviation experiences.

Feel free to contact me at jcgolfer@sky.com

*(Mind your TLAs! As there are many Three Letter Abbreviations in aviation, please refer to the glossary at the end of the book for an explanation of anything that bewilders you.)*

**My CV (no, not the car – that's a 2CV!)**

I started my career as an Air Traffic Control Assistant at Aldergrove Airport, now called Belfast International Airport, in Northern Ireland in May 1973. It was not an auspicious start!

The Isle of Man is an island mid-Irish Sea and a forty-minute flight from Belfast International. My father and I were on the Isle of Man enjoying a bank holiday weekend hockey tournament. My start day at the airport was the following Tuesday. We were due to fly back to Aldergrove on the early evening Monday flight but awoke to find it "harry clampers" – a technical term meaning very foggy and unlikely to clear all day. Great! Dad and I discussed the situation and decided to head for the port of Douglas instead, pick up a boat for Liverpool and then travel overnight to Belfast from there. Of course, that meant I'd be a day late for starting at the airport. Embarrassing, to say the least, but the worst was yet to come. After two boat trips and a restless night crossing back and forward on the Irish Sea, we arrived home to discover that the cars of my fellow hockey players that had been left at our house for the weekend had gone! Yes, the *only* flight to get out of Ronaldsway Airport on the Isle of Man that day was ours! Anyway, it all worked out alright in the end. We'd been in touch with Aldergrove, who said that there wouldn't be a problem starting on the Wednesday.  I really enjoyed my year as an ATC Assistant, watching aeroplanes fly past the window at close quarters – right there, *look*!

1974 saw me in London being interviewed for Air Traffic Controller training to become one of the people who actually throw aeroplanes around. Me! Yes, *me!* Blimey, scary or what? I had books and photographs, all packed into an Air Canada flight bag that Dad had lent me for the occasion, to show the board members just how keen I was on aeroplanes. However, that could well have been a waste of effort because the first half of the thirty-minute interview didn't go at all well. And then the chairman asked me how I had got to London from Belfast. Here's the story of how I began the next forty or so years!

Of course I flew. Checked in for the flight and asked if I could visit the flight deck as I was going for an interview to begin training as an ATCO (Air Traffic Control Officer). The ground staff weren't too sure but suggested I ask when I got on board the aeroplane. And that's what I did.

During the flight and conversation with the Captain, he asked me whether I would like to stay up for the landing. There was *no* way I was leaving the flight deck, I can tell you. What an experience – the first of many as it turned out.

Back to the interview room where the conversation went something like this:

"So, Mr Campbell, how did you get here today?"

"Well, I flew, on a BEA Trident from Belfast."

"How lovely and which runway did you land on at Heathrow?"

"We landed on 10L."

"You seem very sure of that. Are you familiar with the terrain under the approach path of 10L at Heathrow?"

No, not really, but I saw the runway identification marks as we flew over the threshold of the runway."

"Ah, you were on the flight deck. I suppose your station manager set that up for you?"

"No, I just asked if I could visit the flight deck when I got on board."

"A bit of the old Irish blarney eh?"

Laughs all round, and at that point I knew, I just knew, that I'd got my chance to be an Air Traffic Controller.

The next challenge was to get my licence. In those days, the training involved three months at the College of ATC at Bournemouth Airport and then nine months at a unit getting hands-on practical controlling experience. First, though, they taught us how to fly. If we failed to obtain the PPL (Private Pilot's Licence), we would go no further on the ATC course.

What a privilege and an exciting month at Carlisle. On the initial flight with my instructor, I said that coming back into the airport was the best bit. "What, getting back on the ground?" he asked with a dubious look on his face. "No, no, no, flying the approach and the landing," I said. He looked relieved, and after that incident we struck up quite a friendship. Sadly, he was killed in the Danair crash on Tenerife about six years later. He was the co-pilot that day.

After the flying, it was back to college for the first bit of learning – Aerodrome Control (ADC). This is the skill that's performed from the goldfish bowl on top of the control tower – the Visual Control Room. Then back to where I started my career – aerodrome control practical training at Belfast International, under the watchful? eye of Leo Murphy (whom we'll come across later).

After that, back to college for the Approach Radar Control (APC) bit. This is usually on the floor below the goldfish bowl in a control tower, and back then it was in virtually complete darkness because the radar screens were very susceptible to sunlight, which made them nearly unreadable. Not good news when one is trying to keep aeroplanes moving at upwards of 250kts (knots) away from each other! Bournemouth Airport itself was where I practised my approach radar technique during the glorious and unforgettable summer of 1976. What a beach – no, no, I really mean what a beach!

College again in the autumn of that year for the Area Control section of the course. This is the part of ATC that nobody outside of aviation ever sees or perhaps even thinks about. ATC at airports is in sight and therefore in mind because of the control tower, but the en-route ATC centres are well hidden, apart from London Control which used to be based in a housing estate at West Drayton, subtly disguised by thirteen aerials, six radar dishes and three flagpoles! It's now in thick undergrowth just off the M27 in Hampshire. However, I did my Area Control training at Manchester Airport. This was based in the airport's control tower and was therefore easily found!

This was the final part of my training course, and when they asked me, after I had graduated, where I would like to be posted, I said, "If the grown-ups think I'm good enough, I'd like a crack at Heathrow." They obviously did and the rest is history – well, that bit anyway.

Ten years at Heathrow was enough, so I looked around to see where I would like to go. Whoa! It's not that simple. You see, it took a lot of money and time to get me fully qualified at Heathrow, so they (the powers that be) were reluctant to let me out the door. This didn't impress me, and I made two very stupid mistakes. Firstly, I upset too many of my colleagues by being irascible and irrational (my marriage was breaking down and my father figure at Heathrow had retired). Secondly, prompted by nostalgic memories of being the DJ at the local disco, I made an attempt to become the next Terry Wogan and changed career to one which is fickle and mean. Try as I might, I didn't get very far. However, I was a DJ on two radio stations in the late 80s for a few years, albeit with little success and poor pay. During this "mid-life crisis", I knew that I had to preserve and protect my ATC licence and was able to secure a part-time job in ATC at Dunsfold where they built the Harrier and the Hawk aircraft. I'll return to my time at Dunsfold later on.

Show business was not kind to me, so after a while I decided to go back to ATC full time and joined ATC at Bournemouth Airport as its Deputy SATCO (Senior Air Traffic Control Officer). Eight years of light aircraft and middle management took their toll, so I moved to Newcastle – a terrific part of England but *way* too cold for me. Great people, wonderful countryside, fantastic beaches, but... However, I have to say that if Newcastle had been as far south of Bournemouth as it is north, I'd have moved there.

With the need to warm up, I applied for and was accepted as an instructor at an ATC college at Bailbrook, which is near Bath. You won't believe this, but I was there for only four hours when they advised me "with great sadness and apologies" that the college was, in fact, closing in the next three months and that I was therefore redundant! Yep, *four hours*! Surely some kind of record?

Shortly afterwards, I was back where I started, only this time on the other side of the fence, as an instructor at the ATC College at Bournemouth Airport where I had begun twenty-seven years earlier. After a final twelve years, retiring in 2013 was glorious, although I really enjoyed my job and was pretty good at it, which made my working life a lot easier than it might have been had I not been good. How anyone sticks with a job they hate or are no good at confounds me. If that's you, don't wait any longer – get out and do something you enjoy. Never mind the money; you'll get by, no problem.

That's me in a nutshell. Forty-one of my sixty-nine years – not much when you write it down, is it?

# Whirlybirds

When I was a kid, I used to love watching a television programme from the USA called Whirlybirds starring a BELL47 helicopter. What's a BELL47 when it's at home? Well, no doubt you remember the other television programme MASH? The helicopters in the opening sequence bringing in the wounded during the Korean war are BELL47s, the ones with the goldfish bowl stuck onto the leading edge of a piece of scaffolding and sitting on a pair of skis! The definitive light helicopter of the 50s and a magnificent piece of nostalgia. I had the privilege of flying in one, an Army Air Sioux, with the British Army in Northern Ireland just after I started my career at Belfast International Airport, and now I was going to actually get to fly one! You don't believe it? Neither could I, but it's true.

Ron Powell and Bill Booth were pilots for a company based at Bournemouth. It was owned by Bernard and Laura Ashley (the well-known home furnishings guru) and Ron and Bill were the image of Chuck Martin and Pete "PT" Moore of Whirlybirds fame. The company was called All Charter and flew the Bell47 helicopter GBPAI and a Beech Kingair GBJBP. In many ways, this was the real-life Whirlybirds TV programme, which meant that I had leapt from 2D black and white in the late 50s to 3D colour in the early 90s! The lads knew of my love and interest in the Bell, so Ron mentioned that he was flying the chopper to Fairoaks in Hampshire for some repairs and flying back with Bill in the Kingair. Would I like to go along and have a crack at the controls? There's no such thing as a stupid question, but that was pretty close!

Me, get to fly a chopper – a Bell47 into the bargain? Let's go.

6th March 1992 was a gorgeous day, just right for my initiation into how not to fly a helicopter! Flying a fixed-wing aircraft is fairly natural – pull the stick/control yoke towards you, the aeroplane goes up. Push it away, it goes down. Turn it left and so on. A helicopter behaves in a totally different way, but I didn't discover this until we were airborne. Needless to say, Ron did the take-off, or lift-off, to be correct. He didn't let me take the controls until *he* had the beast under control!

The helicopter has three main controls. The stick or cyclic is positioned between the pilot's knees and basically controls the forward and backward and left and right parts. However, when the stick is pulled back, the helicopter tends to stop, not go up! In the other hand is the collective, and it's this which controls the up and down. (It's also got a twist grip which controls the engine rpm.) The third set of controls is at the pilot's feet and controls the torque of the propeller above, using the smaller propeller in the tail as the one above tries to screw us into the ground! There you go, lesson one complete. Easy.

"Ready?" asked Ron.

"Let me at it," I replied. Easy, no danger, piece of duff – yeh, right!

The beast could somehow tell it was me at the controls; it threw its head back and bit my arse, *big time!* Instantly we were all over the place. There's a terrific book titled *Chickenhawk* written by a Vietnam War helicopter pilot in which he describes various hair-raising escapades into dangerous situations. This guy has chopped the tops off trees on his way down into a dangerous landing zone with soldiers on board. He has put the tips of the chopper's skis on a mountain ledge and held it there whilst the weary men climbed aboard. He had an under-slung load which was too heavy to lift directly over an encampment boundary wall so he got the load swinging and it kinda pulled him over the wall! And yet, during his first flight with his instructor, he couldn't control the beast at all. On one early flight, his instructor said, "Right, I've got the cyclic and the collective, all you've got to do is put your feet on the pedals and point us at that tree." After about 15 minutes, the instructor said, "We *are* talking about the same tree, aren't we?"

God alone knows what Ron was thinking about me and my efforts, but he remained impassive and calm, taking back immediate control. He asked me about my flying experience. "Fifty-three hours in a Piper Cherokee," I proudly replied.

"Is that it???" I could see him asking as he looked sideways at me.

"Look," he said, "These things are basically out of control, so the best way to fly it is to imagine it's balanced on a huge beach ball and you're trying to keep it there." What? "OK, come on, give it another go."

He either had the patience of a saint or a death wish for us both. With one hand on the cyclic, the other on the collective and feet on the "rudder" pedals, I climbed on board the beach ball. If it goes left, I ease the cyclic right; if it goes up, I push the collective down. The concentration and muscle tension were tortuous, but I was getting the hang of it. There was a strand of wool on the outside of the bubble which indicated whether we were going in a straight line or not. What wool? I couldn't see anything. We were so far away from a straight line that we were flying virtually sideways, with the wool almost wrapped around one of the skis! We were also going up and down. I was getting the hang of what? Ron took control again and the wool immediately reappeared and stayed in the centre of the windscreen.

We also stopped bobbing. Ron asked what I would like to do next. "Another go?"

I decided to admire the view instead. Thank God for that, he probably thought.

Flying a helicopter is not for cissies, I can tell you. I used to play golf with a helicopter test pilot – I often wonder whether he's dead or in a home for the bewildered!

*The author in his Whirlybird*

# I'm gonna be sick!

The possibility of your throwing up in an aeroplane can depend on quite a few things, for example, being nervous of flying, or the morning after, or a particular flight I was on in February 1976 from Southampton to Guernsey (more on that later). Many of us know that turbulence can make you frightened and therefore cause you to feel sick too. It certainly can, but it isn't dangerous, apart from wake turbulence, which, although potentially violent, is easily avoidable. Wake turbulence is caused by the low-pressure air above a wing meeting the high-pressure air below, resulting in a tight circular airflow from the wings, which then trails behind and below the aircraft like sideways tornadoes. Basically, the larger the aircraft, the bigger the vortex, so we in ATC space lighter aircraft at a greater distance when following a bigger, heavier aircraft. However, in an effort to get more aircraft using the runways at the traffic-saturated Heathrow, a Brymon Airways Captain friend of mine flying from Plymouth in the excellent De Havilland Dash7 suggested that if I could put him right up close to a heavier aircraft on the approach, he would stay above it and therefore out of its turbulent wake! He also said that he would land further down the runway than the previous touchdown and therefore be completely clear of any danger.

A DH7 virtually sitting atop an MD80 looked spectacular from the tower, and it actually worked beautifully, the timing perfect. The powers that be, however, were not impressed, and that was the only time it was tried. (Bet they wish they could do it now at Heathrow!)

Pressurization can cause a feeling of light-headedness and therefore a feeling of nausea, especially at high altitude or if it's not working properly. This is very rare as the pressurisation is closely monitored by the crew at all times. Explosive decompression can scare the bejasus out of you, but it's better not to barf into your oxygen mask if at all possible! So, turbulence, too much alcohol, too much thinking(!) can all cause you to be sick, but the *only* time I've ever felt sick in nearly 760 flights was when holding over Guernsey in a Handley Page Herald, waiting for fog to clear. (Oh, and I was very, very nearly sick in a DC3 Dakota. She was giving "pleasure" flights from Bournemouth around the local area. The Dak fishtailed around Dorset for half an hour and that was plenty! How those WW2 parachutists on D Day survived the flight across the Channel, never mind when they got on the ground, I'll never know. The Dak – beautiful to look at, sounds magnificent, bitch to fly in – at least down the back!)

Anyway, the Herald was a twin-engine aeroplane and this one was ancient! Not that I was worried by that, but it explains why I felt sick! Normally, the pilots are able to use an automatic synchroniser, which keeps the speed and pitch of the two propellers synchronised without having to adjust them manually. This is quite difficult to do successfully and avoid the wha-wah-wha-wah-wha droning caused by the props being out of sync. So, there we were, in calm conditions, with no turbulence. The holding pattern overhead the airport was a left-hand racetrack. Fly for one minute away from the beacon, make a one-minute left turn, fly for one minute towards the beacon and on reaching it, make a left turn, again for one minute. We were in the holding pattern for approximately 35 minutes, which meant we did approximately 9 racetracks – that's eighteen left-hand turns with the engines droning out of sync! Just before we left the hold and set course for Jersey because the fog hadn't lifted sufficiently for us to begin the approach at Guernsey, I thought to myself, "If he doesn't turn right next time, I'm gonna be sick!"

To this day, I've never been sick on an aeroplane. I've been thrown around in an Omani Air Force BA11 during an air test; I've been thrown around in an FRA DA20 being vectored by a trainee at fighter control training school; I've been thrown around in an RAF Hercules while the crew tried to make the SBS trainees in the back sick by pulling the control yoke back and forward, thereby causing positive and negative G forces to be experienced. These are usually guaranteed to make one puke! I've experienced a nasty vortex wake incident in a DC9 behind an Airbus 300 on take-off from Heathrow, quite a violent vortex bump whilst descending into Bournemouth, some heavy-duty winds landing in a BA31 at Southampton, but I've yet to be sick! Crews have tried, airline food has tried, a very steep climb out of Stansted in an empty B737 has tried, copious amounts of Saki, hot and cold, on an All Nippon B747 tried, but no – well not yet, anyway! I hope you are never sick on an aeroplane – it can't be very pleasant for anyone on board.

# 5500 feet straight down

I bet you've experienced hot air. Boardroom, mother-in-law, conservatory salesman, but have you ever experienced a hot air balloon? I've had the privilege on one calm, cloudless Salisbury evening in mid-September 1993. A 40th birthday present and a sheer delight. Just as well it was flat calm as flying a balloon in any wind is no joke; it probably wouldn't have been possible.

I arrived to see the balloon standing upright in a field and ready to go. That basket's bloody big, I thought. I mean there's only me and the pilot, isn't there? Wrong! At around five pm, thirteen – yes, thirteen! – of us were bundled into the huge wicker basket and we lifted off, straight up with the two enormous burners going full tilt. What a noise! What heat! What a wonderful thing to do.

What wind there was as we climbed drifted us off to the south west, but we couldn't feel any wind even though we could plainly see we were moving. Of course, as the wind is moving too, all is calm inside the basket. Well, not totally flat calm as some bodily noises could be heard above the burners' frenzy but no breeze.

We drifted over trees made of sponge, or at least that's how they looked, just like the trees on your train set. (You've got a train set? I won't tell anyone!) We shouted at dogs who wondered where the hell we were. Dogs viewed from above give away the fact that they walk like fish swim. We had a few conversations with people on the ground. I'm serious, low-level flying is wonderful, especially when you're in the open air.

Unfortunately, others on board wanted to go higher. How high? Well, breathable oxygen is just about possible at 20,000 feet but it would be *way* too cold. Our pilot decided on 5500 feet and up we went, burners again on full pelt. That warmed us up no end! We climbed and climbed, and as we did so, it went very quiet in the basket. The noisy "engines" could have blotted out all other sounds, but it wasn't that. Nobody was talking. They might have been enjoying the view and exactly where we were, but I suspect many might have been thinking, "What the hell are we doing way up here in a wicker basket?" Our pilot had told us that if we felt dizzy or sick, just look at the horizon. Whatever you do, *don't* look down. So I looked down! 5500 feet straight down! An interesting and somewhat disconcerting vista. I suddenly had the feeling that the basket wasn't strong enough to hold 14 people! I've never fancied sky-diving but realised that if you want to sky-dive only the one time, you don't need a parachute!! We drifted slowly along with the setting sun, decided to land before it got too dark, picked a field and gently touched down with hardly a bump. Where did we go from there then? We were miles and miles away from our launch site. Did anybody know where we were? Suddenly, three vehicles bedecked with the balloon company's logo appeared, coming up the lane. They'd been tracking us the whole one-hour flight and arrived with champagne and survival, sorry, flight certificates for each of us – how lovely!

Talking of weird flying contraptions, the oddest one I have flown in was an airship, which was basically a barrage balloon with a one-wheeled tin box suspended below it. Within the tin box were four seats, a display of organ stops and a huge wooden wheel, as well as the one engine control. The airship was lit from within every night and sat on the southern perimeter of Bournemouth Airport for about six weeks in the early 90s, advertising Orange, the new mobile phone network. So, it was orange!

"Fancy a trip in an orange barrage balloon?" I was asked. Silly question. Off we went!

With a bloke at the front hanging onto a rope, the pilot started the engine and pulled out some of the organ stops. This action reduced the amount of air in the balloon, leaving the remaining helium, which is lighter than air. The bloke on the rope quickly released his grip, and up and forward we went into a slow and stately climb to 900 feet. We cruised around Dorset for about an hour at a flat-out 50 knots or so, with the pilot turning the big wheel every so often to trim the altitude. It seemed as if we were suspended in space, affording us a glorious view. I would love to travel around Europe in an airship; we felt we were Royalty up there, with everyone we could see peering up at us – what a gorgeously decadent way to fly.

"Anyone for another bottle of Bolly?"

# Now you see it, now you don't (or do you?)

One of the most difficult things to gauge when you're in the air is how far another aircraft is from the one you're flying in. Even highly experienced airline Captains can get it wrong. I was the number 2 (Final Approach Sequence Controller) at Heathrow one gorgeous clear evening. Under my control was a Boeing 747 of British Airways in the descent to 3000ft south of the airport, positioning for runway 28R. He was flying my heading of 070 degrees and descending from FL70 to 3000ft when he suddenly said, "Avoiding action, turning right forty degrees to avoid that 737 directly below me!" That startled me at first until I noticed the aircraft that I think he was referring to. I said that the only aircraft in the sky with him, indeed a Boeing 737, was 4000 feet below! He was most apologetic but swore it was a *lot* closer.

September 1971. Mid-Atlantic at dawn. Aer Lingus 707 FL330 (approximately 33,000 feet) eastbound. I'm seventeen and three-quarter years old and sitting in the jump seat on the flight deck. Just above the cloud horizon, I could see a black blob. As it was only my third flight ever, I asked the Captain, George White, whether it was an aircraft and whether it was coming towards us or going away. He burst out laughing and said, "Yep, it is an aeroplane, but if it was coming towards us, it would be past us by now!"

Fast forward to 10th February 1986. I'm on board a Boeing 737 flight deck of Monarch Airways on a familiarisation flight. (As controllers, we were expected to take two familiarisation flights a year to chat with the flight crews and find out more about what they did and why.) The two Captains that day were flying us from Gatwick to Grenoble. Away in the distance, I spotted a wide contrail coming towards us from about our 11 o'clock position and at the same level. Blimey, it looked as though it wasn't changing its bearing from us, which is a classic symbol of a possible collision! Our two pilots weren't concerned. I saw this thing get closer and closer, but still nothing from the Captains, who had their heads in the office discussing Grenoble's tricky approach procedure. This was in the days before TCAS (glossary), so I was getting a bit twitchy, to say the least. No warning from French ATC – on strike *again* suddenly? Anyway, as you've probably guessed, the oncoming traffic missed us. It was a 747 of TWA and bloody big! It passed 1000 feet below but looked absolutely massive and was away in a matter of seconds as our closing speed was nigh on 1000 knots, give or take. My co-Captains saw nothing!

In June 1989, just after I had arrived to start a new job at Bournemouth Airport, the weather was glorious. Flight Refuelling Aviation (now Draken) has a fleet of DA20 Falcon aircraft, most of which are based at Bournemouth. These little miracles must be made of breeze block as they're over forty years old and still flying today (2022) with Draken. Noisy mind you, the Fan Jet Falcon. I once asked an FRA captain what the most difficult thing about flying a Falcon was, and he replied, "Getting the engines started!" Anyway, FRA frequently offered ATC trips with them, and that day it was my turn. We were flying in a two-ship formation. I was in Blue2, captained by Jez Adamson, with First Officer Jeff Collins. We took off echelon (see glossary) starboard from runway 26 and headed west towards Hartland Point, climbing to our planned level outside controlled airspace. We were behind Blue 1, so Jez said, "Let's see if we can hide from our companion!" Whaaaaaaaaaaaaaat? Yep, hide! That's what we did, right up behind the other DA20 and slightly below! Tell you what, I've looked up the tail pipe of many an aircraft during walkrounds when I've been safely on the ground, but looking up the tailpipe of a Falcon DA20 at 30,000ft is a totally different ball game!

There is a place in aviation called Coffin Corner! This is an altitude where the air is so thin it will not support flight should an engine problem develop causing a reduction in airspeed. If Blue 1 had suddenly had any reduction in power, it would have had no choice but to descend in an effort to stay in the air; we were right up his tailpipe and he didn't know we were there! No wonder Jez kept a sharp eye on him. The plan was to stay there and not say anything until the pre-arranged split to our separate missions. When that time came, I was looking at the instrument panel when Jez called, "3-2-1 split." I looked up and the other aircraft had suddenly and completely disappeared! Gone! One minute there, the next second thin air! We met up again after landing in Culdrose (more on *that* approach later) to refuel for the flight back to Bournemouth, but I was astonished at just how quickly it had disappeared.

Bournemouth ATC, when I was training there in 1976, had an ancient Plessey AR1 primary radar which was very susceptible to anomalous propagation, colloquially known as Anaprop (glossary). Sometimes we could see what we called "angels" – blips tracking across the screen for short distances with no associated aircraft.

We could see hills and waves and birds, too; at least that was what we thought they were. Many times, traffic we were handling had to be given avoiding action on nothing! But the weirdest thing

I saw on Bournemouth's radar at the time was Jersey! Yep, Jersey. It had been very hot that summer for quite a while. These conditions caused the radar beam to be "bent", allowing us to see more distance than we should have been able to. On switching the radar on one morning, there between the Needles and Old Harry Rocks was a perfect outline of Jersey. It melted away shortly afterwards but was quite startling at the time.

Another similar event due to hot weather was an instance at Heathrow. I was handling Heathrow arrivals in the tower and could hear Frankfurt tower loud and clear on the frequency. I called them but they couldn't hear me, which was probably just as well. Who knows what fun I could've had, dealing with Frankfurt airport traffic from Heathrow!

# Big Fat Blob

I'm going to have to be a bit technical for a moment now whilst I explain in some detail what a Big Fat Blob is. In ATC, we use two types of radar equipment. Primary Radar (PSR) is some of the really useful equipment we use to control aircraft. However, it has a lot of drawbacks. It works (and I'll keep this as simple as I can) by blasting out from the rotating aerial you see at virtually every airport a powerful beam of energy into the sky. Anything it strikes will reflect the energy back to the aerial and be subsequently displayed on the radar screen as a big fat blob! Because of the various scales at which the radar display can be set, these blobs can be up to five miles wide! Also, if it is, in fact, an aircraft, we'll have no idea what altitude it's at or passing through, as in climbing or descending. Couple that with different types of airspace, all with differing rules of the air and not all big fat blobs being aeroplanes, things become a trifle awkward. And so it was at Newcastle airport where I had the privilege of working for four years. Newcastle has a very good primary radar, but the airport itself, in my day, was situated in a small pocket of controlled airspace surrounded by an extensive piece of aerial real estate within which various military and civilian aircraft could operate without talking to anyone. All the airliners flying to and from Newcastle had to run the gauntlet through this uncontrolled piece of sky to reach the safety of airways overhead Manchester or Southern Scotland. It was our job to prevent them from hitting anything during the transit. We had to ensure five miles' separation from every "big fat blob", even though it may have been twenty thousand feet above, because we didn't know its altitude or it may not have been an aeroplane at all! Birds, large clouds, trees, even waves could all show up as blobs on the screen. Some traffic had to be flown many more miles than they would've liked, but we had no option back then. Better extra miles in the air than ten seconds inside another aircraft!

There were various ways we could even things out a bit. There were standing agreements on levels and tracks between other units, meaning that the required separation could be guaranteed without the hassle of having to make a phone call to coordinate the situation with an adjoining airfield. For example, aircraft would have to make certain altitudes at or before certain locations and fly at certain speeds at certain times. Standard Instrument Departure procedures, Standard Arrival Routes to airports and agreed separation standards were laid down between units. However, even though the process of co-ordination increased our workload immensely, there were times when it was unavoidable and indeed vital.

The definition of co-ordination is "the organisation of various elements of a complex activity so as to enable them to work together effectively". Fair enough. There were times, however, when I wondered whether the controller on the other end realised what they had said, even though things worked out ok.

South of Newcastle Airport is the very busy military airfield of RAF Leeming in North Yorkshire. Their Hawks and Tornadoes (the aeroplanes, not the natural ones!) were everywhere every day, and the air between us and them was full of fat blobs, so co-ordination was required with Leeming whenever airliners were approaching or leaving Newcastle. On one particular occasion, we were both very, very busy. I phoned Leeming to set up a co-ordination about my southbound B767 level at FL80 wishing to climb to FL190 before joining controlled airspace at Pole Hill, just north of Manchester. The conversation went something like this:

"Leeming, this is Newcastle. Request co-ordination on traffic north of you by ten miles, level at FL80 and requesting climb on track Pole Hill."

The female controller replied, "Newcastle, Leeming, can you see my traffic, bearing from you 240 degrees at 23 miles? He's at FL120 inbound to Leeming."

I confirmed that I could see the traffic and had it identified. Leeming confirmed she had the identification on my traffic and proceeded to carry out the required co-ordination by saying, "Ok, I'll take mine down and you can put yours up."

Three minutes later, she rang again asking for co-ordination on a second aircraft under her control versus the 767 mentioned earlier. After the identification had been confirmed on her aeroplane, she said, "If it's ok, I'll be climbing over the top of you."

By God, I thought, must arrange a visit to Leeming asap. She sounds like a lot of fun! Maybe it was just the heat of battle and so forth.

The other equipment is called Secondary Radar (SSR). This is equipment on the ground which can ask an aeroplane for various types of information including altitude, and the aeroplane can tell the radar. This is a huge step forward for ATC and makes life a lot simpler by substantially reducing the need for co-ordinations.

On another occasion, again at Newcastle, the co-ordination was between the tower controller and Approach Control. It was very clear weather and there was an inbound Shorts360 (a box-like aeroplane with the code SH36, which we nicknamed the "Shed". British Airways also had a few at the time but theirs were known as Conservatories!) Coming from the northwest, they had advised Approach that they were visual with the airport and could join downwind on a right-hand circuit. This was approved by the tower controller, and the aircraft was transferred to her. Immediately, a helicopter called Approach Control, advising that he was flying direct to the airport and approaching from the northwest with the airport in sight. Approach phoned the tower to advise of the helicopter and was asked how close it was. On being told that the helicopter was less than a mile away, and seeing that the Shed hadn't yet turned to a base leg six miles away, she said, "OK, you can come inside my shorts with your chopper."

Really? Yes, that's what she said.

And now for something completely different. A superb example of a lack of co-ordination when it was vital.

Belfast International Airport circa 1973. I had just qualified as an Air Traffic Control Assistant (vital help to the controllers and the best one they ever had – well, so they told me). Runway 26 – it pointed roughly 260 degrees – covered in fog. Thick fog. We could just about see the airport fire station about twenty metres away. A newly qualified tower controller with his first operation in the fog was at the control desk. His only traffic was a Viscount of BEA taxiing out to the runway at holding point Bravo. Runway 26 at Belfast has two holding points where aircraft can hold until they are ready for departure. The holding point at the full length of the runway is called Alpha, and Bravo is an intermediate holding point where smaller and lighter aircraft, not needing the whole length of the runway for departure, usually hold. Bravo is closer to the tower but was still not visible that day.

A phone call from Approach control to the tower controller detailed an inbound BAC1-11 at eight miles from touchdown. The tower controller acknowledged the information, asked the Viscount to report ready for take-off and gave him information on the inbound aircraft. Subsequently, the Viscount called ready and was told to line up on the runway, at which point Approach control advised that the inbound was now at four miles and would be staying on the approach frequency as he would probably go around due to the fog. This was acknowledged by the tower controller, but he omitted to tell Approach control about the upcoming departure of the Viscount. The Viscount was cleared for take-off and told to report airborne. After a short delay, the Viscount's engines were heard passing the tower windows as he called that he was airborne, *at which point*, yes, you've guessed it, Approach phoned to say the 1-11 was going around. The tower controller acknowledged this but again said nothing about the departure! Up went the Viscount through the fog into a gin-clear sky, and round went the 1-11 in the gin-clear sky. Startled as to the position and intentions of the Viscount – it was the first he'd heard of it – the Captain of the 1-11 said, "Ah Belfast, where is that Viscount directly below me going to?" meaning was he climbing or turning or what? This was a perfectly reasonable question in the circumstances and pertinent to the safety of his aircraft. Quick as a flash, the Approach controller replied, "He's going to Leeds!"

I think the tower controller resigned soon after.

In the days after WW2 when radar was in its infancy and wasn't as widely used in ATC as it is now, phone calls about inbound estimates, requested levels and co-ordinations were very common. Later, radar handovers were very common too as a useful way of passing on identification and other information about incoming flights, as well as reducing the workload of the receiving unit and its big fat blobs. There was a classic piece of phone communication in the old days which went something like this:

"Dover, Andover, over."

"Andover, Dover, over."

"Roger Dover. Andover with a radar handover on an Andover from Andover to Dover and he's over Dover, over."

"Roger Andover. Andover from Andover to Dover over Dover, over."

"Roger Dover."

Even the Two Ronnies couldn't have beaten that!

# Simulators
## (some call them Stimulators and I tend to agree!)

Talking of big, fat blobs some trainees we had at the College of ATC were like that. Some of them couldn't tell the front of an aeroplane from the back and had no interest in finding out. The annoyance of meeting people like that is that they robbed a keen person of a place and robbed our company of an employee. Thank God they never got near a real aircraft!

Simulators are very clever machines. Airliner simulators can reproduce almost any scenario that an airline pilot can expect to come across in his or her career, including rare ones like severe turbulence, engine failure, even explosive decompression. Emergencies, poor navigation techniques, cockpit resource management can all be practiced in a simulator to the extent that considerable numbers of newly qualified pilots can take their first trip piloting an airliner with a full complement of passengers on board!

Most airliner simulators these days are of the all-moving type and it can feel quite surreal knowing that you're in a simulator on the ground and yet feeling like you're in a 737 at forty thousand feet. I had the privilege of "flying" a BEA Trident simulator as part of my Air Traffic Control training and it was quite an unnerving experience. Even when we started the engines, they sounded way, way behind us on the flight deck, just as they were in real life.

I remember two fellow ATC cadets on my course teamed together to fly Heathrow – Paris and they were determined to take things as seriously as possible, well one of them was!

All preparations complete and they started the engines. After start checklist, request for taxy clearance, pre take-off checklist, after take-off brief – all perfect. Cleared for take-off and as the aircraft reached flying speed, the "Captain" pulled back on the controls as hard as he could shouting "WEY HEY!" and they crashed at the end of the runway. Roars of laughter from him but total, aghast silence from his "co-pilot" as he reached across and punched the "Captain" on the nose. There followed a huge fight between them and the instructors had to pull them apart! The first case of simulator rage ever. Talk about realism.

Talking of which, I asked an instructor if he would set the simulator up so that we could fly through the worst turbulence ever recorded, just to see how it felt. "No chance," he said explaining that the engineers would be well pissed off as it would have taken ages for them to "repair" the aircraft.

ATC simulators can be used to teach trainees how to throw aeroplanes around the sky safely before going anywhere near a control tower or en-route centre. We can play around with emergencies on the ground and in the air. We can be fighter controllers who try very hard getting aircraft as close to each other as possible. We can be put into situations that will never occur (it says here anyway). I know of a trainee who gave so many headings to an aeroplane on the sim that he actually spelt his initials on the screen – what fun!

However, in my time as an instructor at the College of Air Traffic Control, things were taken quite seriously.

There were EXAMS TO PASS weren't there? Yeh, I know, but ............

I tried VERY hard to do what my instructors had done for me all those years ago – I tried to light the fires of aviation enthusiasm in my trainees. It was my mission to spot trainees who not only were going to be very good controllers but would also turn out to be better than me. I tried to teach the art of ATC, not just the science. Regrettably, It was rare to find a trainee who was keen to practice the art as well as pass exams. However, when I did come across one who was full of the desire to not just pass an exam but also to be a flexible and confident Air Traffic Controller like me, it gave me a deep down glow and a very wide smile.

You know, in my opinion, anyone without a sense of humour has a lack of judgement and should therefore be trusted with nothing. As we've seen, humour plays a significant and vital part in operational aviation and so, believe it or not, here are a couple of examples of humorous events that occurred, even at the College!

The word "Roger" in aviation means: Your message has been received and is understood. So there we were, in the radar sim, which had two positions side by side. Heads down studying the screens and silence in the room as everyone was concentrating so hard.

At one point the instructor next to me stopped the run to explain something to his trainee. She had replied to an aircraft's message using a long sentence with many words, most of which were not required. As an explanation of what she should have said, the instructor said quite innocently, "Well, in most situations, all you need is a quick roger".

We were very busy as instructors and sometimes could be late starting a simulator run. It was up to the trainee to make sure everything was ready before the instructor arrives. For example making sure all the phones were working, the "pilot" was there and ready, the radar picture was orientated correctly. So it was, as I got there late.

"Are you ready for this?" I asked my female trainee.

"I'm gagging for it", she replied.

As I say, an enthusiastic trainee is an absolute delight to train and here's proof. Remember the thlee degree glidepath? 300feet per mile? Apparently many instructors told their trainees that it's easier to multiply than divide. Really? They taught the technique of multiplying the aircraft's altitude by three to calculate the distance required from touchdown. So, according to them, an aeroplane at for example 6000ft will need eighteen miles to run (knock off the zeros and multiply 6 by 3). However, if it descends at the required 300ft per mile, it will end up descending only 5400ft and arrive over the runway 600ft too high! One of the enthusiastic, keen female trainees came to me and said that multiplying the altitude made the descent profile all wrong and she was very annoyed and distressed by it.

"Divide the altitude and what happens?" I said. She made a few calculations from various altitudes, broke into a wide smile of relief and threw her arms around me in a huge hug.

She went on to become an excellent controller at, and an asset to, Birmingham Airport.

In conclusion to this chapter, I must confess to simulator rage myself. In the never-ending search to cut costs that every business seems to embrace, ATC simulators have been developed which don't require "pilots" (the staff who answered the calls from the trainee as if they were real aeroplanes) and so would be cheaper to operate. (Ed : at Bailbrook College of ATC near Bath they placed an ad in the local paper which stated, "Pilots required, no experience necessary, full training will be given". The college was inundated with applicants as you can imagine).

Voice recognition is all the rage these days isn't it? "Alexa, play Classic FM" or "Hey Siri, what's the weather forecast" so why not in a simulator? We instructors had to read into a recorder paragraph after paragraph of gobbledeenonsense until the simulator recognised our voices. It must have had difficulty dealing with my Northern Irish accent because this is what happened on my first try on the new voice activated simulator.

"Virgin 243, request taxy clearance"

"Virgin 243, taxy holding point runway 26"

"Unable"

Wot? Oh, maybe the sim requires the exact and correct phraseology before it can work.

"Virgin 243, taxy holding point Golf runway 26.

"Unable"

Bloody 'ell.

"Virgin 243, taxy holding point Golf runway 26 via taxiway Alpha"

"Unable"

"VIRGIN 243, GO FUCK YOURSELF!!!"

"Unable"

Ah well, that's virgins for you! (my apologies to the real Virgin 243, if there is one!)

# The Manchester Mozzy

During WW2, bomber crews and fighters would often beat up the airfield on getting back from a mission by flying low over the station commander's house or the officers' mess or maybe by doing a victory roll before landing. Many military pilots still do, I reckon, but only at military airfields. However, every so often, a chance comes along at a civilian airport to allow certain "unscheduled" movements to occur. These are a delight for the ATC staff but can cause consternation and not a little anger amongst some of our managers, who seem to readily forget that they were operational staff before they "walked the floor". I hasten to add that the events I will describe were perfectly safe and professionally carried out – they were just a bit out of the ordinary. They don't happen as often, or maybe not at all, these days.

Manchester Airport in 1977 was not the ultra-busy airport it is today, with its parallel runways and big aeroplanes. The control tower was quite small and had a passageway from the door to the control room area, about forty yards long, narrow and quite soundproof too so as not to disturb the control staff. It was therefore unlikely that any of the control staff would hear the door open or people walking along the passageway.

Picture the scene: The control staff on duty had, without management approval, authorised a flypast of the control tower by an RAF Mosquito aircraft. These were twin-engined and used during the Second World War, mostly as pathfinders for the bombers. They flew high and were rarely picked up by anti-aircraft batteries and their searchlights. Their pilots were able to identify a target and "light up" the route by dropping flares. They were unarmed.

Approach control advised the tower controller that the Mozzy, as it was affectionately known, was approaching the westerly end of the runway at low level for the flypast. At that very moment, the control tower door opened and we could hear the SATCO (Senior Air Traffic Control Officer) talking with a VIP visitor saying, "Oh no, we never get anything out of the ordinary here; we're much too busy with… what the f*** was that?" as the Mozzy flew past the tower about fifty feet away, showing a plain view of its underside! Tremendous value for us in the tower but a total shock for the visitors. Later, a shame-faced crew were hauled into the boss's office where knuckles were smartly rapped. I luckily avoided the situation as I was a lowly trainee at the time and therefore totally absolved from any blame. But you know what? I could've sworn that the visitor with the boss had a smile on his face as he left.

One flypast for which I *was* responsible was at Belfast International Airport, again when I was a trainee, but my instructor was asleep so he didn't count!

RAF Aldergrove became the main airport for Northern Ireland when the civil airport at Nutts Corner (what a great name for an Irish airport, eh?) just down the road closed in 1963. However, the RAF and Army Air Corps remained at Aldergrove, so it became a civil airport as well as a military base. Various aircraft were based there, including the Army Air Scouts and Sioux (the military's name for Bell47 helicopters, RAF Varsities and Valettas (we called them flying pigs they were so ugly!), along with fast jets like the Hunter and transport aircraft including Bristol Britannias.

One day, a Hunter was returning from a sortie and asked for a flypast. "No problem," said I. "Your flypast approved." Subsequently, he went around from the flypast down the runway into a right-hand circuit to land.

As he turned downwind, I said, "I've seen better than that."

Whadda mistaykaa to amaykaaa! The pilot didn't say anything; he simply raised the undercarriage. Uh oh, that means trouble! He's going to do it again but a lot faster and probably closer!

The control tower at Aldergrove has a flagpole about twenty yards away and about fifty feet high. Round comes the Hunter, flying at approximately 300kts, and roars between the tower and the flagpole at the level of our windows! "Boss's office here I come" was my immediate thought, but not so. My instructor was still fast asleep and the management team were all at a meeting in the terminal building, which was a mile away. Hooray!

Another one of "my" flypasts was not even close to being as dramatic but was just as beautiful. I was on RAD3 in Heathrow Approach. (Radar 3 was the position which dealt with the many helicopters and light aircraft that flew around Heathrow but never actually landed there. Some did, but they were few and far between.)

Anyway, I wasn't too busy when the Battle of Britain Memorial Flight called for transit of the London CTZ (Control Zone) from south to north en route to their base at RAF Coningsby in Lincolnshire. The BBMF is a formation of three of the most famous aircraft of WW2 – a Lancaster bomber, a Hurricane fighter and the most famous of all, I suppose, a Spitfire. They also enquired if they could route along runway 05. Normally, no chance, but at the particular time they called, there was no aircraft close enough to Heathrow to affect the flypast and the flypast would not have delayed anybody, so I couldn't resist asking the Arrivals controller upstairs if he would like to see a flypast of the BBMF.

"Don't ask silly questions," he replied, so I set it up that they could fly along and just above runway 05. The sound of six Merlin engines as they flew over Heathrow was magnificent; the vision of these three majestic and historic aircraft flying past Heathrow at low level was magnificent; the phone calls from various companies around the airport complaining, "Why didn't you tell us the BBMF was to fly past?" was magnificent. Management didn't stand a chance with any complaint they may have had – even more magnificent!

One other "flypast" is worth a mention as it was so rare! A member of B watch in Heathrow ATC was flying his Cessna172 west to east one day and asked the RAD3 controller if he could fly just north of runway 28R. Usually, this would have been impossible as the delays to our normal traffic would have been unacceptable. For some odd reason which escapes me, there was absolutely no problem! Runway 28R was the departure runway at the time, and I was the departures controller with no urgent traffic to get away. Ron flew his aeroplane just north of the airport, got the view of his life at the place he worked and I got a free pint from him!

# Possibly World War 3.
# Definitely WW2

Ground Movement Control at Heathrow was a very busy place in my day. There are now three GMC positions at Heathrow, but in my day there was only one. With the GMC position in the tower facing north and most stands inside the runway layout, it wasn't too bad from a seeing-what's-going-on standpoint. Most of the traffic was in front of you, but with the opening of Terminal 4 and an increase in the size of the cargo village also "behind" GMC, things could be quite difficult at times, and this lent itself to bits of radio talk that could have caused a major international incident.

I'm pleased to say that most pilots recognise that in ATC, it's first come, first served generally. Mind you, things could be very different should a pilot take exception to a controller's instruction. Such as during the Iran-Iraq war:

"Iranair 202, give way to the Iraqi 747 from your left" or, indeed, vice-versa could have been tricky. Or how about:

"El Al 233 (from Israel), follow the Egyptair 707" or even

"Cyprus 455, the Turkish Airlines is first."

However, one of my faux pas, made completely and totally by reflex, could have been very serious and quite insulting. An aircraft was pushed back from stand A3 and was pointing west on the inner taxiway. Taxiing east on the outer taxiway was a JapanAir 747. The one on the inner called for taxi clearance and I said, "After the JapanAir, nip onto the outer." I swear blind it was a spur of the moment thing, but don't those sorts of things start wars? Talking of which, kinda, here's a story which tickles me to this day.

It was a beautiful summer evening in London. You could see for miles at ground level and a whole stack more when in the air, especially with the street lights on. I've seen it myself, and it's a fantastic sight. Orange and white lights as far as you can see. Another hectic day at Heathrow is winding down and the only traffic consists of a couple of airliners from the German airline Lufthansa, one from Frankfurt and the other from Munich. I'm in Approach Control and vectoring these two onto the final approach for runway 28R. All the usual radio talk involved in getting them into position – "turn right, descend to, turn left, blah blah" – and not too close to each other; don't want a go around this late in the shift.

They are both established on final approach and I'm just about to hand them over to the tower frequency when one of them says, "You know, London, you really haff a very beautiful ziddy."

Before I could reply, the other Lufthansa says, "Vell, you should know, Hans; you 'elped zemm rebuild it."

However, just to balance things a little, there is a story of a British Airways landing at Stuttgart who was told to vacate the runway and taxi to stand 35. The pilot asked where stand 35 was and the controller said, "Vot, you've never been to Stuttgart before?"

"Oh yes, I've been here before, but it was in 1943. It was dark and I didn't stay!"

And one other to complete this section on possible WW3 scenarios. The weather information is broadcast on a loop and is updated every half hour. To indicate the "new" weather, each report is tagged with a letter of the phonetic alphabet, ie A for Alpha, B for Bravo and so on. Aircraft, during their initial call to ATC, tell them what weather information they have, based on the tagged letter.

I was on clearance delivery one morning when an aircraft called, "Heathrow Delivery, this is Pakistan 701; stand J6 request start clearance and we have India."

Just then, another voice said, "Not yet you don't!"

# The thlee deglee glide path

The final bastion of pure air traffic control in these days of automation, computers and fancy gizmos is the Ground Controlled Approach / Surveillance Radar Approach or, as you've probably heard it called, the radar talkdown. Not that the radar does any talking; it just looks out the window. It's obviously the controller who does the talking. Judgement is vital in this procedure and needs the utmost concentration to get the job done accurately and therefore safely. We've already talked about Primary and Secondary radars, and you know the main difference? Good, you've been listening!

For the radar talkdown, you don't need Secondary radar. It may be handy to check the aircraft's progress, but it's not required. Tell you what, we'll switch it off!

Right, primary radar only, with the range set at around 10-12 miles from touchdown.

All we need then is the final approach track marked on the screen, with dashes at every mile. This is done electronically these days, but, and I jest not, when I started my career, some radar screens I came across had the FAT (Final Approach Track – see glossary) marked in white chinagraph pencil (ask your granddad) on the cursor! The cursor was a hard, clear plastic panel over the radar screen which could be spun around a compass rose marked on the console to enable the controller to calculate the required track for an aircraft. Can you believe it? A moveable Final Approach Track – just the job for cocking up the approach, so don't move anything!

Now, the idea is to position the aeroplane so that the "blip" is evenly split across the FAT, pointing in the general direction of the runway (handy that) and at a suitable altitude. I found the most convenient altitude to start the talkdown was 2500ft because at the standard 300ft per mile descent rate, the final approach would begin at around eight miles. (The extra 100ft allowed the descent to get started.) So, we start a final approach talkdown at eight miles and finish at two, or one, or half a mile, depending on the type and performance of the radar and whether it's been approved for that particular use.

Ok, ok, ok, that's the boring bit; now the fun bit. What we say (the phraseology) is written into our manuals and must be used verbatim. This is to keep it consistent and is what the pilot expects to hear so that he can concentrate on flying his aeroplane. Aircraft on final approach descend at roughly 300ft per mile, which equates to a three-degree glide path. Not two degrees, not four, three degrees, the most difficult one to say, especially in the heat of battle, for example, if the call to descend is left a bit late. The number of times I've heard, "Commence your descent now to maintain a thlee deglee glide path."

Alright then, you try it! After embarrassing oneself, things settle down. The main problem is the wind, which veers and decreases as you descend. This means we have to keep adjusting the aircraft's heading to keep him on track (remember: straddling the line), taking into account the changing wind speed and direction. Heading changes can be as little as one degree, which is a tricky thing to fly, especially in a stiff crosswind. An RAF pilot friend of mine says a one-degree heading change in a Vulcan bomber is *impossible* due to the vibration making its compass almost unreadable. He once asked, "Can I turn left 5 degrees and right 4 instead?"

The other thing we have to do is give the pilot distance checks at every mile, with an advisory altitude that he should be at if he's to stay at the required angle of thlee deglees – doh!

So, a sensitive balancing act by both pilot and controller. We practised it often and the pilots seemed to enjoy it too – something out of the ordinary. During my training at Heathrow and before I could take my final checkout, I had to perform 25 SRAs with an instructor and perform one to an examiner's satisfaction during the exam itself. This is how it went.

"Shamrock 233, can you accept a surveillance radar approach for controller training?" I was on the No2 position controlling inbound aeroplanes and putting them on the final approach. Four miles apart, 160 knots. I overheard my colleague sitting right alongside put this to the Aer Lingus pilot and heard him give the pilot the information he needed for the SRA before handing him off to me. Landing runway 28R with a surface wind of around 330 degrees at 20 knots gusting 28. Tricky breeze, to say the least! I was prepared as the aircraft came onto my frequency, and just as I asked him to "establish on the localiser" (this is the Instrument Landing System equipment which he uses to fly an electronic beam automatically towards the runway), he said, "Looks as if the localiser has failed."

I immediately turned him onto the final approach and commenced the SRA. The turn-on was spot on (straddled the line) but as he descended, the wind had a greater and greater effect and I was struggling to find a good heading to keep him "in the pipe".

I must have used fifteen headings during the two-minute talkdown, but he never moved off the centreline – not an inch! At two miles from touchdown and when I said that the approach was complete, he said, "Tanks, that was grand. Right at the runway!"

Roars of laughter as he must have heard my Northern Irish accent and flown the electronic approach, paying no attention at all to me! I'm forever grateful.

Newcastle. One of my fellow controllers there had this theory. As the radar turns clockwise, surely then the beam will scan the aircraft's right wing first when approaching a westerly runway. Therefore, shouldn't we be putting the right tip of the big fat blob on the centreline and not let it straddle? He decided, off his own bat and without any approval, to test this out. And it just so happened that I was on the flight deck of the Brymon Airways Dash8 aircraft when he tried.

"Can you accept a surveillance radar approach for controller training?"

I was thinking, "He's not a training officer! What's going on?"

And then it hit me – he's joking, surely? As it was good weather, the pilot accepted the type of approach. We turned onto the final approach *way* left of the runway centreline and commenced our descent. Not much wind, so our heading was fairly constant – right at Newcastle race course, which is south of the airport! At the end of the approach at one mile from touchdown (Newcastle radar was approved for 1 mile SRAs), we were about a mile left of the centreline and into a hard right turn for the runway!

I knew his theory wouldn't work, the controller in the tower that morning knew it didn't work, yet he went on and on for weeks about it, convinced he was right.

I hope he's staring at a large tropical fish tank and feeling a lot better now.

A very interesting SRA I performed was when I spent some of my training at Bournemouth Airport in the mid-seventies. Because of its generally good weather record, many airlines and the military used to fly there quite often for training. There's a low-level route to the south of Bournemouth which was used regularly by test pilots at Dunsfold, just west of Gatwick. On many occasions, we would get a call from a Hunter routing "St Catherine's, Needles, Hengistbury Head, Wimborne" to skirt around the controlled airspace of Bournemouth's International airport. One time he called, he gave the usual routing and then asked for a practice SRA and go-around with us. No problem, we could fit him in. My instructor said that here was a glorious opportunity to practise on a fast jet. Little did I know just how fast! The pilot then said it would be a practice approach "no compass, no gyro" (direction indicator). Back then, it wasn't unusual for instruments to fail in a military jet, and it was good practice for the pilot. However, it meant that I couldn't use headings to get him down the approach. Now what?

Well, it's normally no sweat with an aircraft doing "normal" speeds, eg 160kts for a jet, around 120 for a propeller-driven aeroplane. We simply tell the pilot to turn and then tell him to stop the turn when applicable. Unbeknown to me, this guy decided to fly down the approach at 300kts! My transmissions went something like this:

"Hawker Romeo, do not acknowledge further transmissions. Commence your descent to maintain a three degree glide path." (Phew!)

"Seven miles from touchdown, your altitude should be 2100ft, on track."

"Drifting left, turn right, stop the turn, six miles from touchdown, your altitude should be 1800ft, slightly left of track, turn right, five miles from touchdown, altitude should be, stop the right turn, turn left, 1500ft, stop turn, four miles from turn, left touchdown, stop 1200ft, three miles altitude should be aaaaaaaaaaaaaaaaaaaaaaaaaaaaaaaaaaaaargh!"

What a mess! A no compass/no gyro SRA at 300kts, but he never told me his speed and I didn't realise until too late! Roars of laughter all round, even from the pilot as he went around and thanked us very much for making his day. Lesson learned – never, *ever* trust a pilot!

There is another type of radar talkdown called Precision Approach Radar. This requires two radars and is therefore primarily used by the military coz they can afford it! One radar scans the approach left and right; the other scans it up and down. The left/right has the centreline marked as on our radar, and the up/down has the glide path marked – at thlee deglees (stop that!). This vastly improves the accuracy of the talkdown and means that the aircraft can be talked right down to the runway threshold. I found this quite hard to believe – no radar I'd ever used was *that* accurate – until the Falcon I mentioned earlier flew a PAR into RNAS (Royal Naval Air Station) Culdrose in Cornwall. The advisory altitudes given by the controller on an SRA are not necessary when flying a PAR because the controller can actually see the aircraft's position relative to the glide path. It's just a matter of advising the pilot whether he's above or below the glide path and to adjust the rate of descent accordingly. The weather was gin clear so it was for practice only, but what an experience. I decided that I wouldn't look out of the windows until the controller said, "Look up and land," at the conclusion of the approach. And there it was, right there, the runway threshold. That's how accurate a PAR is. Now, of course I wasn't flying the Falcon, but I can tell you it's quite a scary thing, even so – actually making yourself disregard exactly where the ground was – wow! One wrong move by the controller and splat! Nerves of steel required all round.

# Where did he say he was??

There are four official languages of aviation – English, French, Spanish and Russian – with English being the most used. Excellent news for us who have English as our mother tongue but not so good for Johnny Foreigner. However, all pilots and controllers with whom I have had contact speak excellent English. Mind you, some accents can catch you out.

The little airfield at Hamble on the south coast near Southampton was a very busy airfield as the British Airways Pilot School was based there. Not only did BA train ab initio pilots there, but other airlines such as Air India used this excellent facility to train their pilots. I visited Hamble one day long after the school was closed and the airfield fell out of use. I swear blind that I could hear the single-engine Piper Cherokees and twin-engine Beech Barons flying all around. Many's the time in 1976 we at Bournemouth ATC would talk to foreign pilots as they flew east and west along the coast during their training. One gorgeous day, I was very busy with light aircraft when an aeroplane from Hamble with an Air India trainee pilot called, giving his position as "overhead Bowleeoh". What? I asked him to say again his position and he replied he had just passed Bowleeoh. Where the hell was Bowleeoh?

I searched a map of the local area but Bowleeoh could not be found. However, *Beaulieu* was clearly marked!

I heard from a friend of mine at Coventry airport that Loog Baroog was mentioned regularly. *Loughborough*!

I often wonder whether, at Hawarden airport near Chester, a call was ever made, "Overhead Bowel Chug Whine." (Bwlchgwyn is a

Welsh village near Wrexham, which is near Chester, which is near Hawarden airport.)

# Where did you say we were?

Back in the good old days, the line that was frequently used on entering a flight deck was, "Lost again?" "Of course," would come the reply.

Navigation back then was usually done by the on-board navigator using what's known as Dead Reckoning. This is where the navigator would stick his head up into a Perspex dome on the roof of the aeroplane and take a sun sighting using a sextant. After plotting the position on a chart and utilising a Dalton computer, which was a bit like a circular slide rule (ask your dad!), he would calculate the heading required to stay on track, taking account of the drift caused by the wind. Not very accurate but at least it served to give a general idea of what was needed. A really good example of Dead Reckoning navigation was called Offset Navigation. Say you were intending to fly to the south coast of England from Scotland. Using the above method, route well to the east or west of your destination on the coast. Then, on reaching the coast, you know *exactly* which way to turn for your destination instead of reaching the coastline and not knowing which way to go. Simple, eh?

Then along came big chunks of metal sunk into the ground. These were the NDB (non-directional beacon) and VOR (very high frequency omni-range) and became the mainstay of aerial navigation for many years. They are still used today at many airports as a useful backup to GPS. There was also Inertial Navigation, whereby the crew entered the aircraft's latitude and longitude position at the start point of its journey. This was known as waypoint 1. They then entered a further number of waypoints up to a maximum of ten, which allowed the aircraft to navigate itself from waypoint to waypoint. The crew would need to be very accurate with the first waypoint to make sure the aeroplane would be where it was supposed to be at waypoint ten! If more than ten waypoints were required, the eleventh would need to be entered after the first one was passed and before the second was reached. Easy to forget, though. One crew on a transatlantic flight omitted to enter waypoint eleven, so when the aeroplane got to number ten, it made a U-turn (typical No 10!) and proceeded back to waypoint one where it started. This was a somewhat startling event for the crew and Oceanic Control!

And so to the present day. Whenever the US military released the GPS for public use, it made navigation very simple. The principle is exactly the same as your car's sat nav. The main difference is that to keep control of where the aircraft are going and ensure they avoid each other, the aircraft still fly along recognised routes, passing through the waypoints designated in the flight plan. However, we don't need the heavy Inertial Nav equipment on board anymore. Waypoints are now named using five letters (at least one vowel), some of which are named after points on the ground, eg BRIPO is overhead Bridport on the south coast. These are displayed on the moving map in front of the pilots, and a magenta line linking them up shows us where we've been and where we're going – handy that!

Some of my favourite waypoint names:

> NEDUL – overhead the Needles off the west point of the Isle of Wight (should have been spelt NEEDL in my humble). The next waypoint is THRED (figures), but some people can't say "th" so it can become FRED, which leads to FRED NEDUL (who's he??).

> DORKI – how dare you call me that!
> (overhead Dorking in Surrey)

NAVEL – about the middle of the North Sea
(Should it be spelt NAVAL?)

LAGER and MILDE – mine's a pint, ya DIPSO (charming!)

DANDI and BEANO could lead to KOMIK.

NAKID – you're either clothes-less or very tired!

SOXON – just west of the Orkney Isles. It's cold there!

DOLOP – at the top of the Peak District
(plenty of snow up there!)

BEWLI – Boleeoh to you and me!

ALLOY – just overhead an oil rig in the North Sea.
(Hope it's made of something stronger!)

GILTI – no comment!

CREWE – wonder where that is?

GINIS and LIFFY – on the way to Dublin

When I was working at Newcastle, the boss asked us for two points around the north east near Newcastle and Sunderland and we came up with:

JORDY and MAKUM (both turned down)

DIKAS – pardon me!

Of course, English language specialists can make up sentences using these names. There's a route in the Indian Ocean which reads:

WHATA BUMMR MOMMA

Others can be strung out together so that a story of sorts is created:

Lord GATER BOWES-BUKEN and his wife Lady MARGO, along with their daughters GERRA and TILNI and their son

GOLES (who had favourite comics the DANDI and the BEANO), fell on hard times and were all living in a CROFT at UPTON, which is near REXAM. They had a DOGGA called SHAPP to add to the ODMIX and every Sunday went to visit the local ABBOT, along with their neighbour TH(f)RED NEDUL, an expert in ARTEX. After the visit, Fred would often say, "I REKNA pint of ADNAM would be grand. Anyone need a lift on my VESPA?"

And of course there are rude ones like:

SUCKS MEDAD BALIX That's not a route; I just made it up, but the waypoints do exist!

There are other nav points worth a mention here. St Abbs is a point in Scotland which is often transmitted by American crews as Stabbs. When the error was pointed out to an American Airways crew, they then asked for a direct routing to Saint Rumble in north Wales. No, no, that one really is Strumble!

More confusion arose when an American military crew asked for a direct track to RAM-BULLIT in France. When the French controller asked whether he meant Rambouillet, pronounced Ram-Boo-Yea, he said, "Well, it's got Rambullit on my flight plan!"

Don't you just love the Yanks?

# The good thing about weather is that it moves. The bad thing about weather is that it moves!

The weather affects all of us. Sir Billy Connolly once said, "There's no such thing as bad weather, only inappropriate clothing." That's true to a certain extent, but flying is *in* the weather, whether in the air or on the ground, and is therefore of enormous interest to a pilot, whether or not he or she is wearing weather-appropriate clothing! Flying in a modern airliner gives us plenty of blue sky, warm sunshine and fluffy white clouds. Most jets fly above the "weather" (clouds) when in the cruise, but getting there can sometimes be "interesting"! There seems to be a built-in desire in pilots to challenge themselves now and then (I think most professionals are the same), but there is also the mantra, "There are old pilots and bold pilots, but there are no old, bold pilots." Also, "An excellent pilot is one who never gets themselves into a situation in which they have to prove that they are an excellent pilot."

Airline pilots used to be a bit gung-ho. They didn't mind taking their passengers through a thunder cloud or taxiing at breakneck speed or allowing the aeroplane to be bumping along in turbulence when a change in altitude would smooth things out.

Nowadays, that's all changed. In these days of corporate liability, aircrews are much more sympathetic towards how their passengers are feeling and will go out of their way to ensure as smooth a trip as possible. Of course, there will be times when it's impossible to be smooth the whole way, but you may notice that the "fasten seat belt" sign is used much more now than in the past, even in light turbulence. Many flights I've been on have been diverted around thunderstorms or even flown completely different, and in some cases much longer, routes to avoid bad weather. A rough flight is these days quite rare.

Weather is also of professional interest to Air Traffic Controllers. For example, have you ever noticed that birds take off and land into the wind? There's a very good reason for that, which I won't bore you with, but it's got to do with the relationship between airspeed and groundspeed. Aeroplanes like to do exactly the same, so the wind direction and speed are vitally important to aviators. Let's have a look at a few of my experiences in the control tower and on the flight deck.

# The wind went right round the clock.

When Heathrow Airport was built, money was no object. It had three sets of parallel runways arranged in a Star of David pattern. The prevailing wind in the UK is from roughly the west, hence runways 28R and 28L – ie roughly into the prevailing wind direction of 270 degrees. The opposite runways, but using the same piece of concrete, were 10R and 10L pointing roughly east. To avoid any nasty crosswinds, 23L and 23R (and their opposites 05R and 05L), along with 33L and 33R (15R and 15L) were built.

There was also another runway near modern day Harmondsworth pointing east/west (ed: I bet the UK Government wishes they still had that other Harmondsworth runway now!!), making a grand total of thirteen runways! No wonder it was known as London Airport, the biggest airport in the UK. However, in my day (1977 – 1987), the 33s, 15s, 05L and 23R, along with that pesky northerly runway, had disappeared. Modern aircraft can cope with stiff crosswinds, but for some reason, runway 23L was still operational. (As I write this in 2022, that cross runway, too, has gone).

9th December 1983, if my memory serves me right, was an extremely busy day at Heathrow's control tower for "A" watch and me. We were on duty from 1400, and the afternoon shift began on westerly runway ops – 28L for landing, 28R for departures.

We knew that the wind was due to back to the south west around mid-shift and weren't at all surprised when the watch supervisor opened runway 23 for landing. This slowed the overall operation a bit in that the landing aircraft slowed down very quickly due to the strong headwind and tended to get embroiled with traffic taxiing to 28R for departure. Sometimes the ground controller had to taxi the landing traffic the "long way round" to avoid conflictions – not popular with aircrew but essential to keep the flow going. No real problems and we soon settled into the routine. However, the weather will do exactly as it likes and had a trick up its sleeve this day which nobody had predicted.

It continued to back in direction and increase in speed, so much so that we had to turn the airport around (not physically, don't be daft!) and began using the easterly runways of 10L and 10R. Because of certain noise restrictions, we had to use 10L for landing and 10R for departures. There was always a period as we changed runway direction when nothing much moved on the airport or in its surrounding airspace, and this slowed the operation even more. I need to digress slightly here because what happened next is vital to this story.

For the moment, let's go flying with a BAC1-11 airliner that day. It was carrying a full load on a flight to Jersey in the Channel Islands. The Captain had taken on some extra fuel for the trip as the winds at Jersey were proving a bit tricky, and it's just as well he did! The runway in Jersey is quite short, and as it is an island, any crosswinds can be ferocious. He held overhead Jersey for just under two hours waiting for the wind to ease a little. This never happened, so he diverted back to Heathrow. So what? Surely no big deal? No, not normally, but today? Wait for it!

Right, back to the tower at Heathrow. Now we're on easterly ops and settling into it quite nicely. Big delays had built up for both arriving and departing aircraft because of having to continually change the runway usage, but we were coping quite well and we kept shovelling!

It was getting dark by now, making things slightly more difficult and a bit tense. The wind continued its backing manoeuvres towards the north east and unbelievably increased its speed steadily. Hard to believe that in the space of about five hours, the wind direction had changed by around 270 degrees from north west to north east – the long way round! There was now a crosswind component on the easterly runways of approximately 40 knots, making arrivals, especially, but some departures too, tricky and potentially dangerous. Concorde had aborted its take-off twice because its small rudder couldn't cope with the crosswind, so the monumental (I'll tell you why in a moment) decision was taken to open runway 05 for landing. Now we're in deep trouble!

Runway 05 did not have an ILS (Instrument Landing System) as it was very rarely used. It also crossed the departure flight path of runway 10R. Because it didn't have the landing system which allowed the aircraft to automatically follow a beam right down to the runway, we had to employ the SRA (the talkdown) to each aircraft. *And* we had to put them the standard four miles apart! This meant we needed two controllers, each giving a talk-down to alternate arrivals. Our workload, which had been pretty high all day, shot through the roof. Approach Control was the busiest I'd ever seen it, with aircraft holding to land, some of them for over ninety minutes. Delays were becoming very long too as the only way to get aircraft onto runway 05 against traffic departing runway 10R was to bring them across the airport from the southerly stacks, run them downwind left hand and fit them in with the northerly arrivals. This led to an extended approach routing and quite a complex traffic pattern.

Back to our friends aloft in the BAC111. Having left Heathrow at around 4 pm for the forty-five-minute flight to Jersey where he held for the guts of two hours then flew about an hour back to Heathrow to be held there for around another hour meant that they had been airborne for roughly four-and-a-half hours to get absolutely nowhere! We brought him off the holding stack and advised him of the extended routing to runway 05, at which point he advised that his fuel state was becoming critical.

Now, we are not permitted to give any aircraft special treatment unless he declares an emergency. No emergency was declared by the pilot, but we were fully aware of what had happened and advised him that he would be number one to land at any time should it be necessary – just let us know. He landed eventually, and on arriving at the gate, the tank was dipped to see how much fuel was still on board. The dipstick was wet only at the bottom! He landed virtually on fumes.

Approach Control may have been ultra busy that day, but it was the controller upstairs in the tower who had the "heavy" job. Because the runway 05 approach path crossed the runway 10R departure path, the departure controller had to look over his left shoulder and gauge the distance from touchdown of the inbound so that he could judge when to give the departure take-off clearance so that the departure was across runway 05 before the lander was at two miles from touchdown! "Shooting the gap" was never easy as we so rarely had to use that method, but it was even more difficult to judge in darkness!

A mighty busy shift finished at 2130 – the busiest shift I have ever accomplished in forty years of aviation. It was the birthday of a friend of mine that day – he wasn't the only one to celebrate! The professionalism of "A" watch that day was impressive and unforgettable. What a privilege to have worked with them.

# Shooting the Gap

The red arrow on the map is a 10R departure / the blue arrow is a 05 lander.

The blue arrow lander should be beyond the yellow star area before the red arrow departure is cleared for take-off. This meant that runway 10R was "clean" of traffic, which it should have been when the red arrow is cleared for take-off.

However, with a further blue arrow lander four miles behind the blue arrow, the red arrow needs to be cleared for take-off before the blue arrow lander touches down so that the red arrow is clear of the yellow area before the *next* blue arrow lander is cleared to land which it wouldn't be because runway 05 wasn't "clean" of traffic because the *next* red arrow had been cleared for take-off!!!!!!.

But, with the red arrow having been cleared for take-off, runway 05 wasn't "clean" of traffic either, as it should have been when the blue arrow was cleared to land!

And so on and so on and so on ..................

Whatever the rules say, the key was to avoid both the red arrow and the blue arrow being in the yellow star area at the same time!

The problems we had to solve were not only what I've tried my best to describe but also the fact that the controller had to look over his left shoulder to see the 05 landing traffic and gauge its distance from touchdown. This was incredibly difficult to do, especially at night. The eyes could easily become "goggled" with double vision as attention to aircraft was split between looking straight ahead at the runway 10R departures and over ones left shoulder at the runway 05 landers - back and forth, back and forth, back and forth! We had a distance from touchdown monitor (a miniature radar screen) which helped but it was slightly to the right of the straight ahead position. Couple all this with having to move the flight progress strips around the board which was positioned slightly below the controller's vision, as well as noting airborne and landing times, then maybe you can see that shooting the gap was no easy task!

Runway 05/23 no longer exists. Kids these days have it easy!

*"Shooting the Gap" (Runway 10R for departure/runway 05 for landing)*

www.mil-airfields.de

# AERODROME
# CHART - ICAO

Highest Elev in TDZ 81
512838 15N 0002824 83W
(GUND Elevation 151)

IRR 110.30°
512838 88N 0002937 08W

Rwy 09L Thr Elev 79
512838 80N 0002906 05W
(GUND Elevation 151)

130

118    103
917    291
634

PAPI
(3.0)
RIGHT 65

ILS GP

MLS
M-HBR
Ch 522

AB13    A13        AB12        AB11    A10W    A10E    A9
        SNAPA    A12     A11

RABIT

COBRA    DINGO        D2    Northern    E2    F2
                                Fuel Farm

Under
Construction

Car Park

Terminal 5A    Terminal 5B    Control
                                Tower    362
                                Fire    129K
                                Station         Pier 7

TSC

Taxiway Y    Twy V

HANLI    DASSO    VIKAS    C1    D1    E1    F1
                  OSTER

MLS                HORKA
M-HRL
Ch 514

100            Disused
RVP            PAPI
West           (3.3)
               LEFT 62

105    N11    NB11    N10    N8    N7    N6
122
101                  NB10    NB8

128    S11                    SB7        SY6    S6

                  ILS GP

I-LL 109.50°        S7
512753 14N 0002928 09W

Rwy 09R Thr Elev 75            Southern        Cargo
512753 25N 0002856 41W        Fuel Farm       Apro
(GUND Elevation 151)                          Cargo
                                              Apron

Highest Elev in TDZ 76
512753 39N 0002816 42W
(GUND Elevation 151)

GUND (Geoid Undulation) =
The height of the Geoid (MSL) above the
Reference Ellipsoid (WGS 84) at the stated position

BEARINGS ARE MAGNETIC
ELEVATIONS AND HEIGHTS ARE IN FEET

| ELEVATIONS IN FEET AMSL | 362 |
| HEIGHTS IN FEET ABOVE AD | 1279% |

| RUNWAY/TAXIWAY/APRON PHYSICAL CHARACTERISTICS | | |
| --- | --- | --- |
| APRON / RWY / TWY | SURFACE | BEARING STRENGTH |
| RWY 09L/27R | Grooved Asphalt | 83F/A/W/T |
| RWY 09R/27L | Grooved Asphalt | 83F/A/W/T |
| Aprons | Concrete/Asphalt | |
| Taxiways | Concrete/Asphalt | |

CHANGE: AREAS UNDER CONSTRUCTION ADDED/AMENDED. TWY B (EAST) EXTENDED TO REPORTING POINT NEVIS. TWY B (SOUTH) TRUNCA

AERO INFO DATE 17 APR 09

Civil Aviation Authority

*Present day Heathrow (note the lack of a cross runway)*

0002741W　　　　　　AD ELEV 83FT

# LONDON HEATHROW
## EGLL

Highest Elev in TDZ 78
512639 30N 0002641 58W
(GUND Elevation 151)

Rwy 27R Thr Elev 78
512639 63N 0002659 74W
(GUND Elevation 151)

MLS
M-HAA
Ch 522

I-AA 110.30°
512639 71N 0002537 49W

VAR 2.1°W - 2009

N

Annual Rate
of Change 0.14°E

ILS GP

Snow
Base

Maintenance
Area 1

Maintenance Area 1

MLS
M-HBB
Ch 514

I-BB 109.50°
512633 86N 0002542 19W

Rwy 27L Thr Elev 77
512753 63N 0002600 68W
(GUND Elevation 151)

Highest Elev in TDZ 78
512753 87N 0002651 38W
(GUND Elevation 151)

ILS GP

| COM | | |
|---|---|---|
| ATIS | 128.075, 115.750, 119.100 (Arrival) | HEATHROW INFO |
| | 121.935 (Departure) | |
| TWR | 118.700, 118.500, 124.475 | HEATHROW TOWER |
| | 121.975 (GM Parking) | HEATHROW DELIVERY |
| | 121.900, 121.700, 121.850 (GMC) | HEATHROW GROUND |
| | 121.600 | HEATHROW FIRE |

| LIGHTING | |
|---|---|
| THR 09L 09R | HI Green with HI W bars |
| THR 27L 27R | HI Green with HI W bars |
| RWY 09L | HI bi-d colour coded CA, TDZ 900m, HI bi-d white edge (first 300m Red), End lights red |
| RWY 27R | HI bi-d colour coded CA, TDZ 901m HI bi-d white edge, End lights red |
| RWY 09R | HI bi-d colour coded CA, TDZ 899m, HI bi-d white edge (first 300m Red), End lights red |
| RWY 27L | HI bi-d colour coded CA, TDZ 901m HI bi-d white edge, End lights red |
| TWY | Green CA and Red stop bars with selective switching on all taxiway routes |

NINGA LINK 31A LINK 24 REMOVED LINK 25 RE-OPENED

# Who's lined up on 28L?

Control tower windows are pretty good nowadays. Big, with no stanchions to get in the way, mist resistant, and some even have wipers. Not so at the old tower at Heathrow. The windows used to mist up quite regularly, sometimes totally obscuring the outside world. Heaters installed did their best but usually were a miserable failure. It had stanchions, too, which one had to peer round at times and a very low roof, which meant one had to bend over and down to see a steeply climbing jet departing. The roof was fine when it was built in 1953 when the majority of aeroplanes were slow climbers, but, for example, a Boeing757 climbs steeply and tends to disappear from view quite quickly. The other problem was heavy rain.

Picture the scene – it's dark, pelting down and busy. 28L for departure with the traffic in the holding bay and the flight progress strips piling up in front of me.

The most efficient way to speed up the departure order back then was to give conditional clearances, for example, "Shamrock 192 after the departing 737 line up."

The rain was so heavy that the holding bay and runway were very hard to see clearly and I was depending on the strip display to tell me the situation outside. Amongst the aeroplanes holding for departure was a rare visitor to Heathrow – an RAF Nimrod, callsign MAC247. Also in the holding bay was IBE504 of the Spanish national airline Iberia. Most of the rest were native English speakers, although the Spanish pilot was very clear too.

Right, let's get the departure order sorted out and get them moving.

"Speedbird 233 after the departing 747 line up."

"Sabena 451 after the departing 737 beside you line up."

"MAC 247 after the departing BA146 line up."

"IBE504 after the departing Nimrod..." I said, shaking my head, "line up."

I was shaking my head because I was thinking that surely the Spaniards wouldn't recognise a Nimrod – and I was right!

"MAC247 cleared for take-off 28L surface wind blah, blah, blah."

Back came the reply, "MAC247 we're still in the holding bay!"

Buggerrit – knew it – the Iberia!

Now I want to make it perfectly clear that I am not blaming the Spaniards.

This situation was my fault. I kinda knew that halfway through the transmission to the Iberia pilot and should really have cancelled the instruction and stopped the transmission. I somehow knew he wouldn't recognise a Nimrod and certainly wouldn't have expected one to be there at all. However, in the heat of battle and all.

Anyway, I now had an embarrassing situation on my hands. I had no idea who was lined up on the runway! I searched through the flight progress strips in front of me but couldn't find any clues as to which aeroplane was on the runway to give take-off clearance to. However, peering through the gloom and heavy rain, I could tell an aircraft was on the runway and ready for departure. Three huge and very bright landing lights pointing roughly in my direction gave it away! I eventually had no choice but to ask the question, "Who's lined up on 28L?"

Hoots of derision from my air traffic control colleagues. "Campbell's lost the picture – ha ha!" Embarrassing, to say the least, but that's all it was – it was *never* unsafe.

There was no reply from any aircraft, never mind the one lined up, so I had to ask the embarrassing question again.

"Who's lined up on 28L?"

More derision, but at last a small Spanish voice said, "So sorree senor, thees es Hiberia 504, we line up."

Quite an admission for him to make because he had disobeyed my order and lined up after a different aircraft. According to the *UK Air Pilot*, the bible of aviation rules in this country, disobeying an Air Traffic Controller's instruction could have landed him in court. At the very least, he expected to hear the words, "Taxi down the runway, vacate to the right and proceed to the holding bay to rejoin the queue." Probably a big delay to him and others while he carried out that manoeuvre. So, I made what I considered to be the best decision and cleared him for take-off. He was so surprised he said,

"Haw kay, Hiberia 504, taking off, muchas gracias amigo!"

Made his day, got me out of a tight spot and saved delays to the other traffic.

Good story, but it gets better! Fast forward roughly thirty years and I'm playing golf in Gran Canaria whilst on holiday. The course at El Cortijo was very busy, so we decided to join up with the two players behind. The conversation got around to what we did for a living, and incredibly one of the two had been an Iberia pilot, and not only that, remembered the incident clearly as he was the co-pilot of Iberia 504 that evening! Small world or what?

# Slush or dry snow – which is safer? If either!

You know that when you walk through new snow it sounds crunchy underfoot and has reasonable grip. During one 36-hour period in the mid-eighties, around six inches of snow fell on Heathrow Airport. We had a considerable array of snow clearance equipment at the airport, which was just as well because we had a considerable amount of snow! The airport authority commenced snow clearance at around midday, attempting to clear runway 28L of snow and make it operational with good braking action and clear of ice and snow. In other words, completely safe for arriving and departing aircraft. Runway 28R was closed due to the carpet of heavy snow lying on it, which meant that all aircraft were delayed, some by substantial lengths of time, some even into double-digit hours. During a lull in the snowfall, the decision was taken to try and clear both runways at the same time. However, the snow came again, even harder this time. Another decision was taken to shut 28R again and concentrate all efforts on runway 28L. All afternoon and overnight, the snow clearance teams slogged on, and eventually 28L was declared open at around 10 am the following morning. *Huge* delays and runway 28R, covered in fine, dry snow, still closed.

Single runway ops at Heathrow will always cause substantial delays to airlines, so a request came through to the tower that a Swissair MD80 be allowed to depart on runway 28R – the one completely covered in snow. We in Air Traffic Control could see no reason why the runway couldn't be used by an airline well experienced in using runways covered in dry snow, but the airport authority refused the request.

Pity as it would have been quite safe and would have looked spectacular! But, of course, if you let one aeroplane depart, others would make the same request and things could then have become quite dangerous. Why? Well, as the runway would have been used by several departures, the snow would have either been compacted into ice or slightly melted into slush, both of which are dangerous and difficult to clear.

Aviation didn't know just how dangerous slush could be until the Munich Air Disaster in February 1958 when the pilot of BEA flight 609 crashed during his third attempt at departure, killing twenty-three people, including some of the Manchester United football team. Captain Thain was blamed for the disaster, but we didn't know then that slush is a real no-no when it comes to airline operations. After the Munich disaster, much research was done to ascertain what effect slush on a runway has on aircraft performance, and this research led to Captain Thain being exonerated ten years later. The research shows that half an inch of wet slush on a runway can reduce the effective thrust of a Jumbo Jet by up to 35% of its power, and just an inch of slush can cause a reduction of 65%! Because of the build-up of slush causing such a reduction in performance, there is absolutely no way in which Captain Thain could have got airborne that tragic night and no way in which he could have known it!

Another potential problem when taking off on a slush-coated runway is that the slush could well attach itself to the wheels and undercarriage, freezing solid as the aircraft climbs. I remember departing in a Brymon Airways Dash8 aircraft from Newcastle on a slush-covered runway and thinking about Captain Thain. Interestingly, the Captain of the flight told us as we were taxiing towards the runway that he would be raising the undercarriage and then lowering it again just after departure in an effort to shake off any slush which had attached itself to the wheels, etc. Sure enough, when he lowered the wheels, huge lumps of slush fell or were blown off the undercarriage. Just as well because if that hadn't worked, we could well have selected the gear down for landing at Southampton and waited for nothing to happen as the slush would have frozen our wheels into the wheel bay. Now that would have ruined at least *my* whole day!

So, dry snow is a lot safer than slush and by quite some way. However, dry runways clear of snow and slush are even safer!

Talking of ice and snow, have you any idea how the crew of a Boeing 757 check for icing? Surely there are instruments on board which can tell? No! Surely the crew can feel any ice build-up? No. Doesn't the aeroplane fly differently if it's iced-up? Yes, but we need to confirm the presence of any ice on board the aircraft *way* before the aeroplane starts to fly differently. So, how? The wings are too far back for a visual check. At night there's no part of the airframe visible anyway. Well, here's how the Captain of a 757, one of the most technically advanced airliners of its time and one on which I was flying into Heathrow, did it. He got his phone, switched on the torch and shone it on the windscreen wiper spigot! I jest not! He shone a torch on a bit of metal sticking up on the outside of the windscreen! It was a bit iced up but of no concern. Effective but a bit Heath Robinson, don't you think?

# What's the wind doing?

As I've mentioned before, birds are clever things. By instinct alone they know from which direction the wind is blowing so that they can turn into the wind for take-off and landing. However, they aren't very adept at landing in a crosswind. Aeroplanes, on the other hand, are, and a skilful pilot can make crosswind operations look very easy when in fact it's a bit tricky – manageable but tricky – if you do it manually. Many airliners' autopilots these days are able to cope with most crosswind situations, but every pilot has to learn and practise the technique during training and refresher flying just in case the autopilot trips out. There are many videos available which show just how tricky it can be (Emirates into Manchester, for example). To mitigate the danger of crosswind landings, airfields like Heathrow had many runways, which eliminated any crosswind problems. Bournemouth, too, used to have a cross runway at right angles to the main one. Runway 17/35 doesn't exist anymore as it was mainly used for light aircraft and training, so wasn't economically viable. It pointed basically into any sea breeze from the south, a wind which can be quite strong, but it was quite short with a road, well, Parley Lane anyway, just off the end. It was rarely used by big aeroplanes, and here's a story which proves the point.

One day, when I was on duty as the aerodrome controller, runway 17 was used by an airliner for take-off. Yep, an airliner! On a runway which, if my memory serves me right, was less than 1300 metres long, which is way, *way* too short for an airliner's use unless the wind is blowing a hoolie! That day it was. 180 degrees 50-65 knots. We'd already seen a Cessna150 virtually hovering over the runway intersection that day, so it was too strong for a crosswind take-off on the main runway (26). The pilot decided to use runway 17 for take-off. As I cleared him for take-off, with the traffic lights on Parley Lane to red, I continually gave him the wind speed so that he could judge whether it was safe to get airborne in the distance that was left of an already short runway. Engines at full power before releasing the brakes, he sped along the runway, getting airborne with just enough clearance of the hedge at the roadside! What a spectacular view of a departing MD80 on climb-out afforded to the queue of motorists and one which has never been repeated. With enough notice of what he was about to do, I could have sold a thousand spectator tickets! If he had suffered an engine failure on take-off, though, it wouldn't have been too much of a problem as he would probably have landed at the Royal Bournemouth Hospital, which is around two miles from Bournemouth Airport.

If you're going to crash an aeroplane, a hospital car park is, in my opinion, the best place to do it.

From Bournemouth to Salzburg in Austria and a story which would fit into the "Why is my flight delayed?" section, but it's got to do with the weather, so I'll put it in here.

I loved to go skiing in the winter months, especially March when the sun's up and the snow can be spectacular. Many people like the winter in the mountains, and the airlines were quick at noticing that market. The Austrian Alps are gorgeous and a delight to ski. Salzburg is the gateway to Austrian skiing and is very busy at peak times. It's also surrounded by mountains to the south, as you can imagine, so the best way into and out of the airport by air is from/to the north or northwest.

The runway is orientated 16/34 (that's roughly 160 degrees and 340 degrees – remember?), so the safest operation is to land on runway 16 towards the mountains and depart on 34 away from the mountains. However, if the wind is such that it makes runway 34 unsuitable for departure, runway 16 may be unsuitable too, and here's why.

We were flying in a Dan-Air BAC1-11 twin-engined aeroplane from Salzburg to Gatwick, departing at around 9 am local time, or at least that was the plan.

The aircraft had arrived from Gatwick on time but it was delayed for the return flight. The reason given to us was a problem with the wind. As there wasn't much wind at Salzburg, I assumed there was too big a crosswind at Gatwick for us to land. However, not so! We eventually did depart (if we never had done, I wouldn't be writing this, would I?) and I visited the flight deck. An interesting story evolved from the flight crew which made perfect sense and provided a reassuring operational reason why we had been delayed. A bit technical, this, but stick with me.

When an airliner wants to depart an airport, depending on its initial routing, it will be given what's known as a SID. Nothing to do with British Gas (remember SID?) but a Standard Instrument Departure, which details the positions of the waypoints or navigational aids that the routing takes it over and the altitudes at which the aircraft must cross those positions. Departures from runway 16 needed to make a fairly smart turn and climb at maximum rate to avoid the mountains and comply with noise abatement procedures. No problem so far. SIDs are constructed keeping aircraft performance in mind, but they only consider that the aircraft flying the SID is fully operational. The BAC1-11 is a twin-engined aircraft and is quite capable of flying any SID. However, planning ahead is vital when operating a jet aeroplane. It would have been folly to take off from runway16 straight towards the mountains and then lose an engine for any reason. That would be half the power of a 1-11 and a dire situation for everyone on board. There wasn't much wind at Salzburg that morning, but it may have been too strong to permit a safe take-off from runway 34. (Even a light tailwind can cause a lot of problems.) In short, we couldn't depart runway 34 because the southerly wind was too strong, and we couldn't depart runway 16 because if we had gotten airborne and lost half the power, we could very well have found ourselves back on the ski slopes inside a vehicle that didn't have skis fitted and without having purchased a ski pass!

# Now don't spill
# the Captain's tea.

"Every cloud has a silver lining." Is this really bad news for pilots? Not in the least.

Cloud itself isn't bad news – usually! A friend of mine was a training captain with a cargo airline called Channel Express. They flew Herald and Electra aircraft and were quite a busy little outfit based in Bournemouth. Jet2 is the reincarnation of Channel Express and still uses the same callsign, "Channex". What's this got to do with cloud? Well, one of the Channel Express pilots said that she enjoyed flying but didn't like flying in CAT (clear air turbulence), so her instructor said, "OK then, fly in cloud!"

Clouds are very interesting beasts and come in many shapes and forms. Essentially, they are just a collection of ice crystals or water droplets. Constantly moving and changing shape, they can often be calming and inspiring; at other times when thunderheads or funnel clouds appear, they can be terrifying. I suppose the "best" clouds to fly in are the strata/layer types. Not very turbulent but amorphous and a bit boring. (There's that "pilots testing themselves" again!) The white fluffy ones you see on a lovely summer's day look gorgeous but can be bumpy, especially as you fly underneath them. However, once you get above the base level of these little beauties, the flying is smooth, as long as you don't go into one, that is! As the summer day unfolds, so the air gets warmer and starts to rise. Towering cumulus (tall, fluffy clouds) develop and, if the air keeps rising, can become the thunder clouds which are also known as Charlie Bravos, so called because the code for these clouds appears on aviation weather reports and forecasts as Cb.

Talking of Charlie Bravos, I have a couple more of my tales from my travels with Brymon Airways. I logged nearly 200 flights with them during my four years working at Newcastle Airport, travelling to and from Southampton Airport.

Commuting, I suppose you'd call it, but a lot of adventures for me. I'm very grateful to all the crews on that route, all of whom were only too pleased to have me on the flight deck when they could.

So, there we were in our Dash8 on a pretty-looking summer's day at 19000ft, all very pleasant and relaxing. Just before we began our descent for Southampton, the Captain said that there was a tall cloud directly ahead. We couldn't climb over it and we couldn't get around it, so we would have to fly through it. Now that gave me an interesting thought as I remembered a pilot friend advising that if you had to fly through a Cb, you might very well exit inverted! I was seated in the back row of the aeroplane, not my favourite place because not only does the aeroplane move much more than at the front but also turbulence is felt more at the rear. I tightened my seat belt and peered out the window. Eventually, I saw the cloud just as we entered it and then *felt* it! We bumped around for about a minute or so, but it felt like ten, and popped out the other side *the right way up – wey hey!*

The other Cb story was in daylight, again with Brymon, on the flight deck this time.

We were flying in dark cloud but only the odd shudder or two, so nothing to worry about. It got darker and darker inside the clouds, and the crew were becoming very quiet, their brows furrowed in concentration. I was studying the weather radar carefully and suddenly noticed a small, solid-looking green blob getting closer and closer. Neither pilot had noticed it, they were pretty busy, but when

I pointed it out to the Captain, he immediately initiated a sharp left turn and advised London air traffic control that we were turning. ATC asked him to say again as the static from the thunderhead had blotted out the transmission. Just as the static reduced, we emerged from the danger, again the right way up, into a cauldron of grey, black and purple which even the witches of Macbeth couldn't have conjured up. I have been a keen observer of the weather since I was a kid, but I've never seen the clouds look more beautiful and more sinister than that afternoon. It looked like what I would imagine Hades to look like! Purple sky overhung with evil-looking black cloud – awe-inspiring and unforgettable.

# Another pesky Charlie Bravo

I arrived at my first posting, Heathrow, having completed my training at the College of Air Traffic Control, on St. Patrick's Day 1977. The evening before, I had checked into a hotel alongside the runway 10L threshold at Heathrow, opened the blinds and said to myself, "Oh my God, what have I done???" Coloured lights and aeroplanes all over the place and as far as the eye could see. Departing aircraft from runway 28R climbing out past my window every minute or so was fascinating but very scary.

One of the controlling skills we were taught at the college was assisting pilots in avoiding weather by using either our Mark 1 eyeball or the radar. Being a young, keen, up-and-thrusting young controller, I was determined to assist aircrew in any way I could when they were avoiding weather. It was to teach me a very important lesson.

Technical stuff again here – please stick with me for a second. Radar in the 70s was pretty basic. We had Primary radar which threw out a beam of high energy and basically bounced off anything it hit and was reflected back to the radar head (the big rotating dish thing). Secondary radar displayed a tag alongside the Primary blip telling us the aircraft's callsign, altitude and routing. One of the drawbacks of the Primary radar was an annoying habit it had of *not* displaying anything moving at a tangent to the radar beam whenever the MTI or moving target indicator was selected. In other words, we didn't want to see hills or masts or chimneys because they didn't move. Any aircraft flying on a tangent to the radar beam was not displayed on the radar screen either because, to the radar, it wasn't moving. All we wanted to see were the aeroplanes.

Right, one wet afternoon and I was just qualified on the radar at Heathrow. A few planes around but it was not overly busy. Much weather showing on the radar, so I decided that the next arrival I was to deal with would be vectored (steered) around the weather, giving the passengers a smoother ride (like I said, keen and thrusting!). So when the next aircraft called, I asked whether he would like to be taken around the weather. "Yes please," he said.

"Fly heading 130 degrees. I can see a lot of weather ahead on your route, but there's a clear patch which I will take you through."

Lots of careful vectoring and I got him in a narrow channel between two Cbs.

At least, that's what I thought! As he left the channel, I told him that he was now clear of the weather and felt really pleased with myself.

"You've just taken us through the worst of it," he remarked.

"What?" I thought. "How can that be??????????" And then I realised what had occurred. The gap was, in fact, a mahoosive, humungous Charlie Bravo which was so big it was hardly moving and therefore had been cancelled out by the MTI and didn't show on my screen!

Needless to say, all further weather avoidance was left to the pilot, and that decision held me in good stead for the rest of my 40-year career!

As an aside regarding Charlie Bravos – just after an evening take-off from Heathrow and passing around 4000ft, we were just about to enter a Cb. Suddenly the windscreen was covered in insects! So that's why sometimes you can see birds close to a thunderstorm. Not daft, are they?

# I can't see a damn thing, can you?

Way back in the 60s when London was blanketed in fog sometimes for days at a time, Heathrow Airport suffered the same fate. Passengers could be stranded there for ages, causing much hassle and annoyance to them, the airlines and their aircrew. Something had to be done and done it was! The "blind landing" was developed whereby aircraft could continue operating even in total white-out conditions. I used to play golf with a BEA pilot who described his first blind landing in a Hawker Siddeley Trident aircraft. "How was it, Keith?" I asked. "It scared the bejasus out of me," he replied and here's why.

The Trident was equipped with a triplex autoland system, well tested and with extensive ground and air training for all potential users. Now, do you know there are various types of fog? No, I never worked for British rail, but this is true! Also, there are two types of aviation fog! There's the type which is gauged from the tower just like you would do from your window. We call that Visibility. The other type of aviation fog is called RVR or Runway Visual Range. This is the distance that the pilot can see from the flight deck windows and can be totally different to the visibility. Depending on the aircrew licence and experience, as well as the equipment in the aeroplane and on the ground being sufficient and serviceable, a successful landing can be made with an RVR of virtually zero. In other words, the pilot can see nothing, nothing at all, nowt!

So, down the approach to runway 28R at Heathrow came Keith in his Trident, being guided to the runway by the Instrument Landing

System. Autopilot on and the triplex autoland system engaged. In front of Keith on the dashboard was a barber-pole-type indicator which moved left and right as the autopilot flew the aircraft towards the ground and upon which Keith had his eyes fixed. Usually, the pilot will arrive at a height on the approach where, if he can't see a visual reference to the ground, preferably the runway, he will have to go around into a missed approach. Keith's decision height was 50ft, and as the aircraft approached this height, the First Officer called, "50 feet, decide."

Keith had already made his decision when they were passing 200ft and said, "Land," as everything looked perfect. He looked up and saw *nothing* – no lights, no runway, nothing. Go around was his first thought, but as the autopilot was still working perfectly well and the triplex was on target, he decided to continue the landing. Just then, the aircraft flared itself for landing and the auto throttle shut off the power to the engines. Keith held his breath. And then felt two soft bumps. The main landing gear had touched the ground. What ground Keith had no idea!

"We could have been in the North Sea, in some fella's back garden, on the M4!" he exclaimed. As the nose wheel lowered, he eventually saw a runway light flash past. And a second and a third, all of them one at a time. He selected reverse thrust and brought the Trident slowly to a stop. He called the tower and said, "Now what do I do???" He couldn't see a thing until a vehicle pulled up in front of him and led him to the parking gate. A scary start to what nowadays is routine and commonplace.

Well done, Keith!

I also have to say well done to Dickie Snell. Dickie was a CAA flight examiner at Bournemouth with vast experience and a wicked sense of humour.

He was also quite generous and would offer trips to any of us in ATC whenever he needed to take a flight to keep his ratings valid. One such trip was to the French seaside town of Dinard. Dickie, his co-pilot and five of us set off first thing. It was beautiful weather for flying and we arrived in Dinard in time for a lovely walk and a very pleasant and extended lunch, for five of us anyway! If you get the chance to visit Dinard, I can highly recommend it. Way too soon it was time for home, so we headed to the airfield and checked the weather in Bournemouth. Fog was forecast! The two crew had a huddled conversation and decided that we should get underway asap. En route up the west side of the Cherbourg peninsula, we were keeping in touch with the weather reports and were hearing bad news. The fog was thickening quite quickly and the RVR was starting to twitch! When I say twitch, I mean that the tower was getting ready to send one of the firemen out to the observation point to count how many runway edge lights he could see. That was the method in those days (early 90s), but now it's automatic, at least at Bournemouth Airport. You can still see the observation point at Southampton Airport, though. As you drive along the M27, you might see what looks like a pair of wooden step ladders and a wooden platform poking up above the hedge. That's the ROP (runway observation point) for RWY02 at Southampton. A person has to stand there for hours on end simply counting how many runway lights he or she can see until either the fog lifts sufficiently to cancel the RVR or they die of hypothermia! (They are usually relieved before that.) The RVR is then calculated from a conversion chart in the tower and passed to the aircraft as a distance in metres from a low of around 100 to as much as 1500. Some of the automatic systems can record down to 25m – slightly less than the length of a heavy goods vehicle.

The RVR at Bournemouth as we flew over Jersey was 1500m. No problem so far because Dickie's minima were a decision height of

200ft and an RVR of 600m.

Any RVR less than that would mean that we couldn't even commence the approach and would need to divert to another airfield. As we passed over the Isle of Wight, the RVR had reduced to 1300 – still no problem and I thought, "That's way above the minimum of 600 we need – over twice as much – so we'll be ok." As we turned onto the final approach at Bournemouth, we were told that the RVR was now 1000m, still 400 above our minimum. A breeze, no sweat, oh yeh? I was peering, peering and peering some more as we descended towards the runway but could see nothing. Surely with an RVR of 1000m, the runway would be in sight well before a missed approach would be necessary? Surely? We were getting close to 300ft (approximately one mile from touchdown and only 100 above our decision height) and still no runway! Suddenly, I was peering into a swimming pool with a disturbed surface and rippling lights down at the bottom. Again and just as suddenly, the runway was in clear view and we landed without any problem.

Believe me, 1000m RVR may sound a lot, but in real life, it ain't!

# The Bovingdon VOR

This is the story of a very sad individual who shall remain nameless to protect the innocent. You won't believe this but it's true, I tell you.

First dates can be a bit tricky. Where shall I take her? Will she like it there? Should it be a surprise? I always played it safe – you know, down the pub or to the pictures or a nice restaurant. But this bloke was an adventurer (or an eejit depending on your point of view), although a bit nerdy.

The big day arrives and so does he, in his Mini, to pick her up. Off they go into the deepest depths of Hertfordshire. "I thought we'd go on a bit of a mystery tour," he tells her. Looking and sounding somewhat unsure, she agrees. It's a beautiful summer evening and she settles in for the journey, to where? Along country roads at first, with friendly conversation and getting to know one another – at least, that's what she thinks. It's getting quite dark and still they travel down smaller and smaller country roads and lanes. Nobody about, no nice pub, little civilisation. She's getting a bit worried now and asks where they are going and how much further it will be. "Not long now," he assures her. Suddenly, he turns left, proceeds up a very muddy track between high hedges and stops beside what looks like a farmer's field. "There it is," he proudly states. She looks around in the gloom and spots something weird in the field. It looks like a space ship and she's wondering whether she's about to be abducted by Martians!

"There's what?" she exclaims nervously.

"The Bovingdon VOR," he says proudly.

What a first date, eh? Sad, don't you think?

PS. This guy had one of the first digital watches in Britain, but he wore a "normal" watch on his other wrist to make sure the digital one worked alright!

# My first flight ever

Do you remember your first steps? Nah. Remember your first driving lesson? Perhaps. How about your first flight? Unforgettable, isn't it? The anticipation of the danger, the sensation of leaving the ground for the first time, the view!

My father had a sister and two brothers, one of whom emigrated with the sister to Canada in the 50s. My grandfather on my father's side died in 1963. This, coupled with the fact that two of her children had "deserted" her, had a traumatic effect on my paternal grandmother. Even after two strokes, she insisted that she fly to and from Canada so that she could be with all her children on a regular basis. She needed assistance with wheelchairs at the airports, support when getting on and off the aircraft, help in getting around the aeroplane. She took it all in her stride, however, and never complained. On one particular journey she was taking in 1971, Dad insisted that I go with her. To this day, I've no idea why he insisted, but I'm eternally grateful that he did. Having left school in June of that year and not beginning college until October, it was the perfect slot in my schedule to experience what was to become a lifelong delight and the start of a love affair and my career, although I wasn't aware of that at the time. My careers master at school, Mr Maximillion Gillespie (what a great name), had drawn my attention to Air Traffic Control, but as it was then part of the Civil Service, I hadn't paid it much heed. He also taught maths, including geometry, and during class one day, as I was watching the BAC 1-11 flight inbound from Birmingham to Belfast International airport, he said, "Concentrate, Campbell! You'll get nowhere in life looking out the windows at aeroplanes." "But sir, I'll never use geometry ever again!" I'm very pleased to say that we were both totally wrong! I owe Max Gillespie so much; I'll never forget him.

I digress. Where was I? Oh yes, being "forced" into going to Canada with my grandmother. We were booked on an Aer Lingus 707 from Belfast to Montreal via Shannon. The flight was only about half full so we pushed back from the stand on time. I was waving out the window at Mum and Dad in the terminal, just as I'd seen passengers do on other visits to the airport. To me, the people in the aeroplane always looked so small and vulnerable and a bit frightened as the aircraft taxied away. And I was now part of their ranks. I felt small and vulnerable too but not frightened in the least. Excitement was what I felt. We taxied for quite a long way in a buffeting wind and eventually took off from what I now know was runway 35 into a stiff northerly breeze and therefore, initially anyway, going in the wrong direction! Man, what a feeling as the powerful 707 climbed steeply away, making a split-arse climbing turn towards the south west with the north of Ireland slowly becoming laid out below me. Up like the glass lifts on the outside of tall buildings. Straight up! At least, that's how it felt to me.

I can't remember the rest of the flight, the landing at Shannon, the take-off at Shannon or the landing at Montreal, but they must have been successful!

All I remember was that first take-off, fifty years ago as I write this. I've experienced over 750 take-offs since that heady day, but nothing beats that first one, not even when I got to land a light plane for the first time on my own a few years later.

I clearly remember that landing, but nothing comes to mind re the take-off.

Life's weird, isn't it?

PS. I lie! I do remember one other item from that journey. The one and only time ever that my baggage went missing was on that flight! We changed aircraft in Shannon, and the one which flew from Belfast went on to New York with my bag! I haven't had any luggage go missing since, not once in over 750 flights – not bad going, eh?

# Who can it be? Surely not!

It's dark and quiet and peaceful. At least it is on the Cyprus Airways A310 flight deck. The APU (Auxiliary Power Unit – an aeroplane's extra engine) is running to keep the lights on in the cabin, but the flight deck is dark and virtually silent, with only quiet conversation about the upcoming flight. We're sitting at the gate in Larnaca Airport, Cyprus, waiting for start clearance. ATC is going ballistic! The radar at Nicosia centre is unserviceable and traffic is being controlled without the use of radar – this is known as procedural control. Larnaca's radar is also out of service. Nowadays, this is very rare as there are numerous backup systems both at airports and control centres. Back then, in 1991, and at some smaller airports these days which don't have a radar, separation between aircraft is achieved using various navigation beacons along with timings, speeds, altitudes and one very efficient separation which can *only* be used in daylight. Procedural control is just as safe as using radar but very s-l-o-w! So, although radar is not necessary for the safe control of aircraft, not being able to "see" the traffic makes life a bit 16th century – not that Henry VIII ever flew, but hopefully you get my drift!

"Cyprus 952, Larnaca Tower, start for London approved, report ready to taxi."

All five of us on the flight deck sit up, belt up and I, for one, shut up! The Captain flicks a switch and suddenly we can't see outside! (This is why your crew dim the lights for take-off and landing in the dark – that way, should anything untoward happen when you're on the ground, you've got the necessary night vision.)

This sudden appearance of the multi-coloured lights on the flight deck is quite a sight, I can tell you, and leaves a lasting impression.

"Larnaca, Cyprus 952 ready for taxi."

"Cyprus 952, follow the Malev Airlines 737 from your right." (Malev used to be the national airline of Hungary.) At walking pace, we taxi to the runway and await our ATC clearance. In the meantime, the Malev ahead of us has been given clearance: "After departure, turn left on a direct track for the Chekka VOR, climb FL90 (9000ft), be advised that radar is out of service." Hungarian he might be but the pilot's English is pretty good and he reads back the clearance perfectly and also acknowledges the lack of radar available. His destination is Tel Aviv, hence the left turn off the westerly runway at Larnaca.

"Cyprus 952, after departure, climb on track the Paphos NDB FL70." My first thought is why FL70? (The Malev ahead is climbing to FL90, so why not FL80 for us after he has passed FL80 in the climb? FL80 is a westbound level and we are to be tracking west. Also, 1000ft is the vertical separation standard. We find out later.) The first officer reads back the clearance and also acknowledges the lack of radar. So far, so good. Another separation standard we use is once one aircraft has passed a beacon – in this case, the Larnaca VOR – and is going in the opposite direction, the "other" traffic can be climbed through his level.

The Malev is cleared for take-off and we observe his left turn as he climbs away. ATC ask him to report on an easterly track from the VOR which he quite quickly does but then asks for a radar heading! The controller advises that this is not possible, having no radar. The Malev doesn't reply, and suddenly I'm a bit concerned. If the Malev can't find the way to the Chekka VOR, he could become a big problem to us! However, we're cleared for take-off. ATC are now using VOR separation as the Malev has still not passed through our assigned level but is confirmed as being east of Larnaca – maybe lost, we'll never know! Personally, until I was convinced that the Malev was not a problem to us, ie on track to Chekka, I would not have issued our take-off clearance. (I cross my fingers and keep a sharp lookout for a possible rogue Boeing 737!) However, our take-off clearance comes, so we enter the runway, check that everyone's ready and off we go, west towards Paphos. I'm hoping for the best, although the Malev is long gone!

It's cloudless and moonless and pitch black as we set course for Paphos and are handed over to Nicosia control. We now discover what's at FL80. About a minute or so after we level at FL70, Nicosia Control asks whether we can see a Hercules aircraft on our starboard (right-hand) side. I look out of the windows and see only a flashing red navigation light, but not necessarily a Hercules and not necessarily at FL80. To my astonishment, the Captain replies that he can indeed see the Hercules! You're having a laugh, I think. Remember back at the beginning of this chapter, I mentioned a separation standard which could only be used in daylight? Remember also that Nicosia had no serviceable radar, which meant they couldn't see either of us. So, to expedite our climb, the suggestion is that we can use this visual separation method by seeing the other traffic and climbing through its level. Quite a safe manoeuvre in daylight but fraught with danger at night. Never mind – we are cleared to climb, maintaining our own separation from that "Hercules", and so we do! To this day, I often wonder whether that aircraft really was a Hercules or something else. If it was something else, what? Was it at FL80?? It could have been the Malev!

Thinking about it now, I reckon Nicosia was using the radar at RAF Akrotiri to monitor everyone's progress, so there was really no danger.

# Controlling without
# the use of radar

This is achieved using mental gymnastics involving speeds, timings, levels, position reports as well as various beacons and turning points. Many have compared it to three dimensional chess – with the pieces all moving at speeds of up to 200kts!

As you can see, it's a bit ancient but was used by the ATC colleges for many years. Most airports these days have radars but they can be turned off for maintenance, or indeed fail altogether so trainees needed to learn this type of controlling. It was one of my favourite disciplines and is called Approach Procedural Control ie control of aeroplanes using laid down procedures/separations.

What I'm looking at is a flight progress board using plastic strip holders in which are pieces of paper roughly 8 inches long and an inch wide. These flight progress strips were legal documents and so had to be written on legibly. I took great pride in doing this carefully, neatly and accurately – a work of art! Nowadays, flight progress strips are electronic.

The four strips in the middle section of the board are the "live" ones and represent the aircraft under my control. The yellow strip-holders are the inbound aircraft and the blue holders the departing traffic. The strips on either side of the middle section are pending traffic. The screen to the top right shows the actual weather at the airport and the yellow buttons to the left are various telephones.

Concentration is vital when controlling aircraft but applying procedural control does sharpen the mind a bit more. However, the overall flow of air traffic is substantially reduced without the radar so there's a little bit of thinking time necessary to select the right tool for the job.

"What separation can I use between these two aircraft??"

Much laughter as I was learning. I often had two aeroplanes at the same place at the same level at the same time! It's a simulator and I eventually got the hang of it, you no doubt will be pleased to hear!

*The author controlling aircraft without using radar*

John Campbell

*GBRYA - a DeHavilland DH7 - the greatest STOL (short take-off and landing) airliner ever built*

*The Manchester Mozzy*

*A VOR*

*PAR (precision approach radar) hardware*

John Campbell

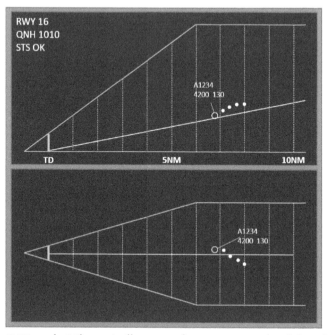

*PAR - what the controller sees. The top screen is the glidepath /
the bottom screen is the left/right (azimuth)*

# Example of SRA phraseology

Bigjet 123 this will be a surveillance radar approach to runway 26 terminating at two nautical miles from touchdown, check your minima, step-down fix and minimum descent height.

Bigjet 123, one zero miles from touchdown, turn right heading 260 degrees, final approach.

Bigjet 123, niner miles from touchdown, check gear.

Bigjet 123, slightly right of track, turn left two degrees heading two fife eight

Bigjet 123, eight miles from touchdown, commence your descent to maintain a three degree glidepath

Bigjet 123, on track, 7 miles from touchdown, your height should be two one zero zero feet

Bigjet 123, right of track, turn left three degrees heading two fife fife, six miles from touchdown, your height should be one eight zero zero feet

Bigjet 123, drifting right, turn left two degrees heading two fife three, fife miles from touchdown, your height should one fife zero zero feet.

Bigjet 123, four miles from touchdown, slightly left of track, turn right two degrees heading two fife fife, height should be one two zero zero feet, cleared to land runway 26 surface wind two three zero degrees one eight knots gusting three two knots.

Bigjet 123, three miles from touchdown, your height should be niner fife zero feet, turn left two degrees heading two fife three, check minimum descent height.

Bigjet 123 on track, two miles from touchdown, the approach is complete, out.

*(using the Precision Approach Radar notice the difference – check heights are not given. The controller will say for example "slightly above the glidepath, adjust your rate of descent.*

*Hence the title "Precision")*

# Trans World Airlines (TWA)

*Caption*

TWA was a major American airline which flew from 1930 until 2001. It was founded and owned by the legendary Howard Hughes (who designed the Spruce Goose – so called because it was made of wood, a bit like the Manchester Mozzy! – and was the pilot on its first and only flight). TWA was formed as Transcontinental and Western Air to fly a route to LA from New York via St. Louis, Kansas City and other stops with Ford Trimotors. It was based at John F Kennedy Airport and eventually flew international links with London, Paris and Frankfurt, to name just a few. American Airlines bought TWA in 2001 and ended an era of flight crews who were always "up for a laugh", although always very professional and cool.

Here is a selection of radio exchanges between me and them which I hope will raise a smile.

The Shorts 360 was built in Belfast, Northern Ireland. It had a square, box-like fuselage and square stubby wings, was twin-engined and was affectionately known as a Shed. Some had the view that it was towing a caravan! One morning, I was on Heathrow Departures on runway 28R. I liked 28R for departures because it had plenty of intermediate departure points which could be used to expedite the flow of departing traffic, and most smaller aircraft would use these points quite regularly. However, at that particular time, the ground controller was very busy, so most aircraft were told to use the full length of the runway for departure to avoid blocking any taxiway.

The runways at Heathrow used to have mahoosive holding bays in which we could shuffle the departure order to give the most efficient flow, and in the bay was a Shorts360, a Shed, sitting beside a TWA747. It came the 360's turn to depart, so I cleared him to enter the runway and line up. To the TWA I said, "After the departing Shorts360, line up 28R."

He said, "Is that this blue one beside me?"

"That's the one," I replied.

"Be nice when they get it out of the box!" was the retort.

The Breguet Deux Ponts is probably the ugliest aeroplane you're ever likely to see, although the Varsity and Valetta were very close seconds! Study the photograph carefully and you'll see what I mean. Two tails, four engines, two decks! At any rate, a rare visitor to Heathrow. He was parked on what were the Lima stands in my day and just around the corner from the Kilo stands cul-de-sac. The Limas were adjacent to the inner taxiway at Heathrow, so aeroplanes pushing off those stands blocked the taxiway to other aircraft. And sure enough, a TWA747 was on the move in his direction! The Breguet was given push-back clearance and was sitting on the taxiway going through the after-engine-start checklist, which took quite a while. Round the corner from the Kilo cul-de-sac came the TWA. I said to him, "Follow the Breguet Deux Ponts ahead of you to the holding point runway 28L."

He said, "Is that this little pig thing in front of me?"

At which a tiny little French voice said, "It might look like aay peeg but eet fly like a burd."

Take that, ya big meanie!

This one is an absolute cracker! I was the Heathrow Arrivals controller and had with me a young student from a local school who was on a work experience day. I was showing her the kit we used (wind speed and direction indicators/distance from touchdown monitors/ground radar display/frequency selectors) amongst other items, and she was looking really bored and fed up with her time in air traffic control. I thought I'd cheer her up a bit by allowing her to talk to an aircraft if she wanted to. (Note – due to licensing requirements in this day and age, what I'm about to describe is not allowed anymore, even for non-ATC people who may have a VHF radio licence.) She was a bit frightened by this but decided she'd give it a try.

We rehearsed the phraseology, eg "Speedbird (BA) 123 cleared to land runway 28R surface wind 240 degrees 14 knots" and she became quite proficient. Watching and listening also helped prepare her for the big time.

I now have to digress for a moment to explain an integral part of the phraseology above. In my day, when the surface wind was less than 5 knots, we would simply give the wind direction and say that its speed was less than 5 knots. However, after an incident at Gatwick involving a Continental Airways 747 which had been given the wind as 320 degrees less than 5 knots and on just getting airborne had a No1 engine surge and subsequent failure, things changed. The aeroplane was very heavy and proceeded to fly around dumping fuel so that it could be at a low enough weight to be landed back at

Gatwick, in the process affording the passengers an excellent view of West Sussex! (I know this because there was a friend of mine on board at the time.) The incident was attributed to the inaccurate wind speed information given to the pilot on departure by ATC, so we now have to say the exact wind speed, even if it's only one knot, which is just over 1mph!

Right, back to Heathrow Arrivals and my "trainee". I needed to select a fluent English-speaking pilot to make sure she could understand what he was saying. Cedarjet from Beirut, Air China from Beijing, Alitalia from Milan wouldn't be clear enough. Good English they all speak, well, maybe not Air China, but English is not their mother tongue. I spotted a TWA coming round the corner onto final approach and thought, "Perfect!"

"Ready for some work experience?" I asked my protégé.

She looked petrified! The aircraft made his initial call with me and I told him to report the outer marker (that takes some of you back, I'm sure!), approximately four miles from touchdown. I turned to my assistant and said that when he called passing the outer marker, to go into our little routine and clear him to land with the wind information. He called and she bravely and nervously said, "TWA 704 clear... cleared to land runw... runway 28 right the surf... the surface wind is 270 degrees... at two knots." Phew, not bad! Hesitant and a bit high-pitched with nerves but all the words in the right order. Quick as a flash, TWA 704 replied, "Copied the wind London; is it gusting?"

She – went – bright – red! I burst out laughing. What a great story.

There's another TWA classic involving very cold air and a very hot-headed female controller in Oceanic control at Prestwick. You've probably heard of the 777 which crashed at Heathrow in 2009 due to fuel starvation caused by the extensive cold air experienced when flying from Beijing to London. Well, a TWA flight was crossing the Atlantic Ocean one winter's night from Los Angeles, a long flight passing just south of the North Pole. As we know from the Beijing experience, prolonged cold air can cause the fuel to begin to thicken, even solidify if the exposure is for too long a period. On leaving Oceanic airspace, the aircraft called Scottish Control and advised that they wished to descend as soon as possible due to the cold fuel.

"Standby," came the curt reply from a weary female controller.

A further five minutes went by, and the pilot again asked for a descent.

"Standby, I said!"

After a further short period, the pilot yet again asked for an urgent descent as the fuel was getting quite cold now and risked solidifying.

"STANDBY!"

Immediately, he said, "Gee, Ma'am, was I ever married to you?"

TWA – sadly missed.

John Campbell

*"Nice when they get it out of the box" A British Midland Shed - BA called theirs Conservatories*

*"It may look like a peeg but it fly like a burd" Breuget Deux-Ponts*

# Tall tales and wee stories and all true!

Cast your mind back, if you will, to the Cyprus Airways flight from Larnaca in Cyprus.

You remember, the one with the "Mystery of FL80"? Anyway, I had arranged for a friend of mine in Heathrow ATC to pick me up from the airport after we'd arrived. Unbeknown to me, he had gone into work and was monitoring my progress on the radar. Suddenly, the Captain was asked by Heathrow Approach if I was on board.

I was sitting in the flight deck jump seat just behind him, so leant forward with my thumb up. He was a bit startled by this, which doesn't surprise me, because he knew I was there but didn't know my name. He quickly replied that I was indeed on the flight deck and listening in.

"OK, can you advise him that his driver is waiting?"

Before he had a chance to reply, an Aer Lingus popped up on the frequency and said, "Can I have a driver too, please?"

And immediately another somewhat posh voice said, "You don't get paid enough to have a driver!"

One evening, whilst working in Newcastle Approach control, I discovered a friend of mine, Brian Bibb, on the radio as co-pilot on an inbound British Midland 737. They were positioning in empty to fly a ski charter the next day and he suggested that I could come with them as there was an empty seat. No hesitation from me, so off we went the following day to Turin in Northern Italy. Brian was doing the flying, and as we descended over the Dolomites, the Captain asked what his intentions were regarding the approach. Now Brian is a speed merchant, so we were fair chugging along. No problem with that, but if you don't get the speed off in good time, the mass of the aircraft and its inertia can get a bit difficult to control, meaning the speed will be slow to come off and one can end up too fast and/or too high at the runway threshold. This would possibly require a go-around from the approach, with the subsequent fuel burn and probably a late departure for the flight home. So Brian started to tell the Captain his plan.

"We can see the airport and the mountains, so I'm going to fly down to the MSA (minimum safe altitude) and then turn right for a downwind join of the runway. We'll wait until we are clear of the mountains and then ask for a further descent at that point."

"Very good," replied the Captain. "What's the first thing you're going to do?"

"I've got the ILS set and the cleared level, so I'll ask for descent very shortly."

"Fine, but what's the *first* thing you're going to do?"

"Uh..." Brian looked at the Captain, bewildered.

"You're going to SLOW DOWN!"

We were doing around 340kts at the time, as I remember, and Brian looked a bit crestfallen as the Captain disengaged the autopilot and reduced the thrust. However, our valiant First Officer recovered his composure and later flew the perfect approach, topped off with a flawless "greaser" landing.

The next leg of the journey was to Stansted. Uneventful and another gorgeous landing by Brian. The Captain then decided to fly the final leg from Stansted to Heathrow. The aeroplane was empty, but still, he cocked up the flare on landing at Heathrow and we came to taxi speed only after two glorious bounces! Was Brian pleased or what? (Only joking.)

The De Havilland Dash 7 is a remarkable aeroplane and the *only* one that was approved to land at London City airport when it first opened. The aircraft's STOL (short take-off and landing) capabilities are extraordinary. I've had the pleasure and the privilege of being up front twice in a Dash 7.

The first time was arriving at Plymouth Airport. We were about a mile from touchdown at around 1000ft (normally this would have meant a go-around as we were *way* too high) and the Captain asked me whether I thought we'd make the runway. No chance! 1000ft one mile from touchdown – what, are you crazy?

All he did was select the huge lift dumpers along the top of both wings. We fluttered down to the runway, flared for the landing and then main wheels – dink, nose wheel – dink and we stopped virtually immediately on the runway! Fabulous and impossible in any "normal" airliner.

My second experience of the Dash 7 was even more spectacular. Southampton to Newcastle. Strong westerly wind at both airports. Southampton's runway is quite short. It has a taxiway holding point halfway along the runway, and most aircraft need to backtrack (see glossary) the runway if departing to the south for a sufficient run to enable a successful take-off. We arrived at this holding point, reported ready for take-off and told the tower, "We'll take it from here." I can imagine what the tower controller was thinking. "There's no way he can take that for take-off – there's not enough runway." Sounding very uncertain, he cleared us for take-off and we used only about 200 metres of the runway before we were airborne – unbelievable and it gets even better.

Approaching Newcastle, we received the weather information, which included the wind direction and speed of 270 degrees, 25 knots gusting 40, Runway 25 in use.

I noticed the two pilots look at each other and then the Captain looked over his shoulder at me and said, "How about runway 07?" I couldn't believe my ears!

Now listen carefully because we're back into technical stuff for a moment. *Any* wind behind us for take-off or landing will increase the length of tarmac we need to use by quite a large amount. Even a five-knot tailwind will give us serious problems.

As for twenty-five, never mind forty, forget it! However, approach control approved us to use runway 07 for the landing.

More technical stuff for a moment. Runway 25 at Newcastle has only one turn-off from the runway and it's a fast turn-off, by which I mean the taxiway is a "Y" junction instead of a "T", which means that on runway 07, it's a reverse "Y" or an upside-down "V". (I hope you can picture that ok).

Down the approach we went with the final wind check 270 degrees 27 knots. The Captain flared the aircraft over the threshold in preparation for the landing. Main wheels – dink, nose wheel – dink and we just missed the turn-off! A twenty-seven-knot tailwind to use less than a quarter of Newcastle's "opposite" runway – what a machine!

An early morning shift for me at Heathrow. Fiddled about checking the weather, checking any work in progress on the field, grabbed a cup of coffee and wandered into the approach control ops room where I was scheduled to work for the shift.

Now let me tell you, there's nothing worse than having to work hard at the end of a nightshift when you're bursting to get out the door on your way home and waiting for the fresh morning shift to appear through the door. But the end of this particular night shift and the beginning of my morning shift had a bit of a twist. As I said, I wandered into the ops room to see my fellow Irishman, Kevin Staunton, gesticulating wildly in my direction.

"John, John, get over here quick!"

He was alone in the room, so I supposed he needed urgent help as the traffic had built up. I rushed across the room and plugged my headset into the radar position beside him.

"What are you doing?" he asked. "It's not busy, but I need you to take over from me right now!"

I looked at him questioningly (is that a word?) but he was getting quite agitated, so I unplugged his headset and sat in his seat. As he bustled out of the room, I asked him whether he was ok. Was he sick?

"No, no," he replied.

"What, then?"

"Oh, I've got to rush down to stand B6."

Now I thought he was late for his flight back to Ireland and wished him a safe journey.

"On no," he said, "it's just that I bet the Aer Lingus pilot (who was on a visual approach and therefore flying the approach without any directions from ATC) a fiver that he couldn't turn onto the final approach at less than two miles." This is a very close turn onto the final approach to an airport for an airliner! Doable but tight.

He had lost the bet. What a character!

As part of my duties as an Air Traffic Controller, I was expected to take two familiarisation flights a year on my days off. I'll talk a little more later on about some of these, but this one from 1982 sticks in my mind.

Gatwick – Naples – Gatwick on board a Boeing 737-200 of Britannia Airways, the forerunner of present-day TUI. We were in Naples discussing the engine failure procedures just in case something untoward happened on departure. Most crews discuss this kind of thing before they start the engines so that they both know what to do in the event that an engine fails just after lift-off.

The engine-out procedure was this: full power on the good engine, maintain 2000ft if possible, fly around Mount Vesuvius (!) and land back at Naples. Simples.

As we were taxiing out, the Captain suggested that we fly the first half of the engine-out procedure and therefore not reduce power after getting airborne. Also, we would not maintain 2000ft or fly around Mt Vesuvius, but we would not fly the noise abatement track either. So, basically, full power on both engines and a bit closer than usual to a block of flats just south west of the airport. I asked, "Won't there be complaints from the residents in the flats?"

The captain replied that they would be so busy selling ice cream that they wouldn't even notice us! We got airborne on full chat and shot past the windows of the flats. The noise must have been deafening, and I mean DEAFENING, as the 737-200 engines were probably the noisiest in the world at that time. I often wonder whether any complaints about us ever came in to the airport in Naples.

ATC had a computer. When it worked, it was invaluable! The trouble was that it used to not work quite often! And when it didn't, all hell would break loose. ATC delays would build up very quickly, all traffic coming to a standstill at times. And so it was one week in the late 70s. The computer had been slow most of the week and there had been a couple of outages, meaning all traffic had to stop temporarily.

Normally, there would've been over forty departures every hour at Heathrow, but on my departure frequency that morning, there was a lone 757 of BA taxiing to the runway. Yep, all one of it. So I thought I'd cheer him up a bit.

"Fancy a good laugh?" I asked.

"I could do with a good laugh," he said.

"Well, there are two IBM9020D computers in the UK. We have one up here, and the science museum has the one that works."

Here's another true story, this from my time at Bournemouth Airport in the 90s.

All the Royals back then, when actually flying an aircraft, had their personal callsigns. These have all been removed now for security reasons, so it's safe to tell this story.

Prince Andrew's callsign was Leopard. However, the Prince himself never spoke on the radio. That was always done by the co-pilot, who was from the RAF with a minimum rank of Wing Commander. We received information that Leopard would be flying from London to Portland in a helicopter at 1500ft and would pass through Bournemouth's area of responsibility. No problem, it was a regular occurrence.

Now Prince Andrew and I are keen golfers (not that he knows that, of course), and he had just been appointed as Captain of the R&A. Leopard duly called and was given all the appropriate information. I was able to monitor his progress on the radar and an idea came to me. We were forbidden to transmit anything other than the required information to the aircraft but, after much thought and pacing back and forth, I decided to give it a try.

"Leopard, Bournemouth."

"Pass your message Bournemouth."

"Congratulations, sir, on your appointment as Captain of the R&A, and can I have it after you?"

That's it, I thought, I'm done for. However, a reply came back so quickly it could only have been Prince Andrew himself!

"No," was what he said.

Luckily, I've never been inside the Tower of London, but it was a close-run thing!

Have you ever listened closely to any announcements made by the Captain on your flights? Here's First Officer Speed Merchant again, except that now he's a Captain. Just after the Channel Tunnel was opened, Brian Bibb, again on a British Midland 737 from London to Paris, made his mid-flight information call to the animals (that's what pilots call us, the passengers!). It went something like this:

"Ladies and gentlemen, this is your Captain speaking. Just over the English coast now and climbing to twenty-three thousand feet. The weather in Paris is warm with a gentle westerly breeze. Hope you're enjoying this short flight with us, and those of you on the left side of the aircraft have a tremendous view of the newly opened Channel Tunnel." You know what, I bet everyone on that side of the aeroplane turned to look down, *and* I bet a few on the other side also went over to have a look!

And then, the same thing happened to me (he said, embarrassed). Unbelievable but true, and I haven't lived it down since.

Back in the mid-nineties, a charter company at Bournemouth airport ran "chimney pot check" flights for children at Christmas time. This was billed as a Christmas family treat but was really only a short flight around the local area. To fill the aircraft to impress the public and therefore sell more tickets for subsequent flights, empty seats were offered to airport staff. Being the naive person I was at the time, I thought, "Why not? It'll be a bit of fun and a chance of another flight for my logbook." I got on board virtually last, to be confronted by hordes of screaming children accompanied by parents and grandparents – the noise was ear-shattering. I should have gotten straight off the aeroplane there and then, but I couldn't resist another flight. "It'll be ok; once we get airborne things will calm down." Yeh, right.

As the engines started, the kid in the seat in front of me went berserk! Wouldn't fasten his seat belt; screamed like a stuck hyena. Might have been frightened, I suppose, but boy, did he let rip, and he didn't stop the whole thirty-two-minute flight.

Anyway, we at last got airborne and straight into layers of cloud – couldn't see a thing. The crew were very good at grabbing the children's interest, though, and now we come to the point of this story.

"So, everybody, what we are going to do now is look out of the windows and see if we can glimpse Santa's sleigh," came the announcement from the cabin crew.

I promptly looked down at my lap and began studying the carpet and the seat table in front of me. This went on for quite a while, when suddenly one of the cabin crew exclaimed, "Oh look children, there it is! There's Santa's sleigh!"

And what did I do? You've guessed it. I looked out of the window! Doh!

I'm forced to reveal this to you only because a colleague of mine at the time was sitting two rows ahead of me and on the other side of the aircraft. He looked up too, but he was looking at me!

All I could think was please, please, get this thing back on the ground.

Back to a short story about an airline Captain who avoided not only a crew safety issue, a possible flight delay with consequent overnight hotel accommodation for his passengers and a fine for breaking the airport night jet ban quota, but also a visit to his chief pilot's office without tea and biscuits. The only people to cotton on to what was happening were the flight deck crew of Captain, First Officer, Flight Engineer and... me!

The flight in question was a gorgeous DC8 operated by Arrow Air, an American airline, and flown by Captain Peterson, a person with a superb southern USA drawl. One could imagine him sitting in the captain's seat wearing studded cowboy boots and a huge Stetson, smoking an enormous stogie and playing his geetar!

The aeroplane was to fly from Miami about half full and pick us up in Tampa before travelling on to Gatwick. On checking in at Tampa, we were informed that the aircraft would be two to three hours late departing.

Now, virtually every airport in the world tries to be a good neighbour by limiting the number of jet aircraft that can fly into or out of it between the hours of 2300 and 0600 the following morning, and as our original departure time of 2000 (8 pm) was tight anyway, this delay meant that we would be pushing the jet ban time limit.

The aircraft eventually arrived at Tampa with about forty-five minutes to be airborne or stuck overnight. We were asked to be as quick as possible taking our seats, which, to my surprise, we all did, and the engines were started with about fifteen minutes to go to 2300. There was a slight problem getting the tug, which pushed us back off the stand unhitched, and we proceeded to taxi at a fairly brisk rate, you might say, certainly a stack faster than the recommended "fast walking" speed. As we approached the runway for take-off, the

Captain came on and said, "Cabin crew, take your seats for take-off, and that includes Janet!"

Which means that the aircraft got airborne from Miami without one of the cabin crew strapped in. Oops, but it could have been very nasty as the cabin wasn't secure.

Anyway, my thanks to Captain Peterson and his crew for getting us into Gatwick just about an hour late the following morning.

Way back in the late 70s, the Royal Air Force of Oman had some of their aircraft and pilots based at Prestwick in Scotland. Even though Prestwick is right on the west coast of Scotland, it has a pretty good weather record, and this particular day was gin clear. One of the Omani planes called for taxi clearance on a sortie out over the North Sea at high level, and as he was on the move, the Prestwick controller called Scottish Military Control for the clearance.

"Muscat 90 is cleared to enter North Sea high level at or above FL290 (29,000ft). Frequency after departure will be VHF 132.85. Can he make FL290 by the coast?"

The Prestwick controller then asked Muscat 90 whether he could make the required level, and the pilot said that he probably could.

Subsequently, the aircraft was cleared for take-off. He throttled up to full power, released the brakes and off he went, virtually straight up! Within no time at all, he called, "Just crossing the coast climbing through FL220 (22,000ft) and sorry didn't quite make the level."

On passing the airborne time to Scottish Control, along with the information that the aircraft didn't quite make the required level by the coast, there was a stunned silence on the phone. Then a voice said, "Noooooooooooooo, I meant the east coast!"

Talking of the Oman Air Force, here's an interesting wee story, if not very funny. It requires a pre-amble, which can be boring, but I'll keep it as short as I can.

Every time an aircraft wishes to fly along an airway, it must file a flight plan with Air Traffic Control. The bits of information on the flight plan which we require are the aircraft's callsign, type, speed, altitude it wishes to fly at, its route and its destination.

(If necessary, other information we could access included the flight duration and the amount of fuel on board, as well as the planned diversion airport and what type of survival equipment it carried.) From this information, the computer would produce flight progress strips for the tower, as well as all the sectors the aircraft was to pass through on its journey.

The Omani Royal Flight was a regular visitor to Heathrow in the 80s. It was a Douglas DC8 with the registration A40-HM, which was written on the side of the aircraft just as on any other aircraft. The registration can be used as the callsign as every aeroplane in the world has its own "name" and is therefore unique, avoiding any callsign confusion. If, for any reason, the aircraft is withdrawn from use, its registration cannot be used by another.

Back then, there were many ATC delays due to increasing traffic wishing to use the most popular routes across Europe, but, as always, pilots and operations departments were, and probably still are, adept at getting around these problems. The way to solve a particular delay was to re-file the flight plan along a different route with fewer/shorter delays, and this the Omani Royal Flight did.

A40-HM had had its original flight plan submitted along a route which would mean a two- to three-hour delay on departure, so it was decided to go a different way and a new flight plan was filed. To recognise that a new flight plan had been filed, the original flight plan had to be cancelled. And the way that the newly formed Flow Control Unit knew which one had been cancelled was that the new one had to have the letter "Q" added to the callsign.

Are you still with me? I don't believe you.

Anyway, the ops department of the Omani Royal Flight had not added the "Q" to the new flight plan callsign, and after a confusing half hour or so whilst we frantically tried to find out which route he intended to use, the aircraft was eventually cleared to taxi to the departure runway.

Now, I further have to explain that an Ulsterman talking to an Omani and getting his message across clearly can prove to be tricky, and this indeed turned out to be the case. As he was taxiing, I tried to explain as best as I could that the next time the flight plan was changed, he needed to use the callsign A40-HMQ.

Guess what happened? The next time the aeroplane arrived at Heathrow, written on the side of the DC8 were the letters A40-HMQ as the aircraft's registration! Doh!

# It's beginning to sound a lot like Christmas?

Surely, in forty years of working shifts, one is bound to have to work at Christmas a fair bit? Well, for some reason or other, I only ever had to be at work once during a festive season. Yep, only one Christmas afternoon, ever!

Most regional airports, eg Bournemouth, Southampton and Exeter, are closed on Christmas Day. The bigger ones such as Manchester, Heathrow and Newcastle are open 24-7, albeit usually quieter than normal.

Back in the late seventies, early eighties, there were four controller positions in the tower (the goldfish bowl bit) at Heathrow: Clearance delivery, Ground movement control, Departure control and Arrivals. When things got quieter, we used to bandbox the frequencies, eg departures and arrivals would be on the one frequency. It was so quiet that Christmas afternoon that we had all four control positions bandboxed onto one – me!

At one point, I had not one aeroplane on the frequency! At Heathrow! Hard to imagine these days. I thought, "How are we going to liven things up a bit?" Here's what I did.

There is normally a crowd of aircraft spotters at Heathrow. They used to congregate on the roof of the Terminal 2 car park and became a regular sight at the airport. The Queens Building was also a popular spot, so much so that it used to have a kids' roundabout on the roof! Anyway, I wondered whether any spotters would be listening to Heathrow on Christmas Day – surely not? I pressed the transmit switch and said, "Hello and a very Merry Christmas. If you're listening to this and would like a dedication this Christmas day, phone this number. Can't play any music but I can say hello." I had given them the number of the watch supervisor's desk in the tower, and you won't believe it but the phone rang! And then it rang again! And twice more! For Pete's sake, we couldn't believe it ourselves. People were actually listening to Heathrow on Christmas Day!

Here's some advice if one of them was you – get out and get a life!

# Some pilots are really stupid, others are just stupid, others just sound stupid.

"Pushback approved, face east."
"Which way's east?"

Flying is really not that difficult once you suss it out. It's got simple instructions which anyone can understand. Trouble is that there are scrillions of them! However, if you take it at a reasonable pace, there should be little problem in learning at least the basics. Like this – pull the stick back, the houses get smaller. Push it forward, they get bigger. What could be simpler? It's not *that* easy, c'mon.

Being an Air Traffic Controller has the same ethos. If you can divide by three and add sixes, you'll have no trouble being an airport approach controller. Why? Ask any of us. Divide the altitude of the aeroplane by three to ascertain the distance that the aircraft will need in order to be at runway elevation when it gets to the runway! Handy to know so that your immaculate vectoring doesn't get him over the runway threshold too high! Then add sixes so that he will be six miles behind the one ahead. Easy. If you don't know your three and six times tables, don't even apply for ATC training.

You'll need to be reasonably fluent in English too as it's spoken around the world. Now I don't mean upper-class, posh English but aviation English, a language all of its own. For example, this was a short instruction to a helicopter wishing to cross a busy runway.

"GCLLE, cross runway 26 at the intersection, expedite, inbound traffic at five miles on final approach."

"G-LE, cross runway 26, roger."

He fiddled about and fiddled about a bit more until the exasperated controller said,

"G-LE, cross runway 26, EXPEDITE."

"Roger, G-LE is crossing." S-l-o-w-l-y, s-l-o-w-l-y, s-l-o-w-l-y.

"G-LE I said expedite; go as fast as you can!"

"G-LE roger, why didn't you say that in the first place?"

Aaaaaaaaaaaaaaaaaaaaaaaaaaaaaaaaaaaaaaaaaaargh!

More examples of stupidity – what were they thinking??

"What's your endurance?"

"Oh yes, we're fully insured."

"G-UB report at three miles."

"We've passed three miles."

"Roger, what's your range?"

"Three miles."

WOT?

"Heathrow, GBAIG overhead Denham unsure of my position."

"Bournemouth, what's the position of that rain shower at the end of the runway?"

"What's your flight time?"

"Not really sure, but we should be away an hour."

"Go around, I say again, go around, Cessna on the runway."

The aircraft landed and went around the Cessna on the runway.

Stupid? Might have been my fault.

"G-UZ, how do you read my transmissions?"

"3700 feet on the Tyne regional." (That's the pressure setting.) WOT?

"Manchester, Shamrock (callsign of Aer Lingus) 123, passing FL80, cleared to FL100."

"Shamrock 123 Manchester, Climb FL180, report your assigned heading."

"Shamrock 123 climbing FL180, afraid I've forgotten the assigned heading but it will be the one we're presently flying."

Good old Aer Lingus, always there to raise a laugh.

If a pilot ever says to you, "Understood," don't believe him. I say again, do *not* believe him.

"Bournemouth Tower, good morning, CHANNEX 125, can I check the weather?"

"Channex 125, Bournemouth, good morning, surface wind 260 degrees 12 knots, visibility 5000 metres in haze, cloud scattered at 1000 feet, temperature plus 8, QNH (air pressure at sea level) 1015 millibars, runway 26 for departure."

"Roger, understood, can we have the wind again please?"

"Surface wind 260 degrees 12 knots."

"Thank you, and the temperature?"

"Plus 8."

"Roger, the visibility and cloud...?"

"5000 metres in haze, scattered at 1000 feet."

DON'T!

"And the pressure, please."

Aaaaaaaaaaaaaaaaaaaaaaaaaaaaaaaaaaaaaaaaaaaaaaaargh!

"Roger, understand we're No1. Is there anyone ahead of us?"

Back in the 70s, British Airways used to do a lot of crew training at Prestwick Airport on the west coast of Scotland, mainly because of its runway length – over 10,000 metres – huge! One sunny afternoon, up comes a BA 707 for training and tells Prestwick approach control that he has the airport in sight and wishes to carry out a visual approach. Now, just off the coast is the island of Arran, and on that island which is under the final approach to the long runway is a fairly substantial piece of real estate called Goat Fell – a mountain nearly 3000 feet high.

"Speedbird 12 Tango, cleared for a visual approach to runway 13, caution Goat Fell 2866 feet."

Roger, Speedbird 12 Tango, cleared for a visual approach to runway 13, copied Goat Fell, is it a danger area?"

"It will be if you hit it!"

When I started out in my aviation career, the equipment on the ground and in the air was a *lot* less sophisticated than it is today. Most of it was clockwork and easy to read – big dials with needles; some of it was digital and computerised, and it was this information which was of tremendous use to us back then. For example, the speed of the wind and its direction at 2000ft was invaluable in allowing us to judge the best headings during a radar talkdown, and we asked for it regularly from the newer airliners like the Boeing 757.

"G-FG what's the wind at your level?"

"We're heading 230 degrees."

"G-FG, I say again what's the wind at your level?" "We're at

7000ft."

"G-FG, I say again, WHAT'S THE WIND AT YOUR LEVEL!?"

"Oh, the wind is 43 knots."

"Any direction?"

"From the front."

Gawd 'elp us!

To a light aircraft who called out of the blue one day at Bournemouth:

"Request your point of departure?" (Meaning where did he get airborne from.)

He replied, "Well, it's a nice day so I thought I'd go flying."

"Morning Teesside, can you give me a rough time check?"

"It's Monday."

"Glasgow Tower, this is Cessna 152, do you read?" No reply.

"Glasgow Tower, this is Cessna 152, do you read?" No reply.

Same again and again no reply.

At which point the instructor said, "Shall I try calling them on *my* stopwatch?"

"Morning Leeming, can you give me a time check? Thanks."

"Who is requesting the time check?"

"What difference does it make?"

"It's very important."

"*What*?"

"Well, if you're a flying club pilot, the time is 3 o'clock; if you're

RAF it's 1500 hours; if you're Navy, it's 6 bells; if you're Army, the big hand is on the 12 and the little hand is on the 3 (that's me in *real* trouble, even though I'm only kidding!); if you're Marines, it's Thursday and 120 minutes from Happy Hour; and if you're a Business Jet pilot, you can afford to buy a watch!"

Pilots! ATC would be a great job if it weren't for pilots. They are a bunch of strange beasts, sometimes creative, sometimes canny, sometimes downright annoying! There was, until recently, an annoying habit amongst some of the younger pilots of picking up American slang radio phrases, which not only threatens aviation safety but can be confusing. "Roger that" is most annoying. American films use it all the time. Just "Roger" will do to acknowledge a transmission. "Can I get ......." is heard all the time in bars and takeaways - ugh! But the real crazy stuff originates, I believe, in the US military. Get this.

Heathrow to Glasgow. Clear day, autopilot on, nothing to spoil the Captain's day. Until he's on the approach into Glasgow. The tail didn't fall off and the engines didn't fail or anything serious like that, but it was the First Officer's remarks when it came time to put the undercarriage down that surprised and annoyed the Captain.

"Shall I dangle the Dunlops? Zebra crossing coming up fast." (Those are the markings on the runway threshold.)

The customary "Gear down," replied the Captain, appalled at what he had just heard.

The undercarriage locked into position and the lad said, "Boots on and laced. The freight dog at the end of the road has made his left," meaning the preceding landing aircraft had vacated the runway. Apparently, the young pilot had done most of his training in California and had picked it up there. Dealing with foreign pilots can be a problem in standard aviation English, as we'll see later, but add in a load of hip talk and we're heading for trouble.

It's even worse in the US military, by all accounts. What should have been a simple call of

"Tower, this is Airforce 558 at 8000 feet, 15 miles straight in approach, request touch and go" became "Tower, this is chrome-piped stovepipe double nickle eight ball, angels eight, fifteen in the slot to bounce and blow."

The tower replied, "Roger, you've got the nod to hit the sod!"

Blimey, we'll all be killed!

**Most pilots are clever and some of them are very quick!**

Over the years, I've heard many quick retorts on the RT from pilots and indeed controllers. Here is a selection of ones I've used, ones I've heard and ones I've read about. There's a website if you'd like to read some others. It's called PPRUNE – give it a try.

ATC - "Clipper 124, what's the turbulence like at your level?"

Clipper 124 - "Not sure how to describe it, but the Captain has just had his fork stuck up his nose."

ATC - "Shamrock 43, what's the turbulence like with you?"

Shamrock 43 - "Can't tell, we haven't eaten yet!"

Me - Channex 988 (male crew), cleared for a visual approach to runway 17, you're number one, in fact, you're the only one."

Channex 988 - "Roger, cleared for a visual approach to runway 17 and I'm the only one, thank you, darling!"

ATC - "Flyer 65C, I had you number one but you're now number two to the 737."

Flyer 65C - "Oh, you big bully!"

Me at Heathrow. Runway 28L for landing. An Air France Boeing 727 just touching down with an Aeroflot (national airline of Russia)

close behind.

Me - "Aeroflot 242, continue approach, expect a late landing clearance." No reply.

The Boeing is braking hard, but I judge he'll miss the fast turnoff and prepare to send the Aeroflot aircraft around.

Me - "Aeroflot 242, continue approach, a 727 to vacate."

Me - "Aeroflot 242, go around..." (Just at that point, the 727 makes the fast turnoff, so clearing the runway.) "I say again, you're cleared to land."

He probably wasn't listening anyway and was landing no matter what.

ATC - "For noise abatement, turn right 45 degrees."

A/C - "Confirm for noise abatement, we're well clear of the coast over the sea!"

ATC - "Confirming for noise abatement. Have you ever heard the noise a Cessna makes when it hits a Nimrod?"

A Douglas DC8 makes a very heavy landing. Waiting for departure is a microlite aircraft, which is basically a hang glider with an engine. Home-made, of course.

As the DC8 leaves the runway, the pilot cheekily remarks, "Nice little machine you have there. Did you build it yourself?"

"I did, out of old DC8 parts, and if you land like that again, I'll have enough to build a second one!"

Most aircraft altimeters are calibrated to show an altitude based on a pressure setting expressed in millibars. However, most Americans use the pressure setting in the old money of inches.

ATC to an American aircraft, "Descend to 3000ft, the pressure setting 1022Mb."

American – "Roger, can we have that in inches?"

ATC – Roger, descend to 36000 inches, the pressure setting is 1022Mb."

Expletives and obscenities are to be avoided on aviation radio. However, it was a very busy day, with aeroplanes stacked up for departure. The wind changed direction, so they all had to taxi to the other end of the airport to enable a take-off into wind. As the first one in the queue got to the other end, the wind changed back again.

"Shit!" was heard on the radio.

ATC – "Who said shit?" (a fatal mistake) BA – "It wasn't us. Dreadful!"

Air UK – "We wouldn't say shit either."

Pan AM – "Well shit, we sure as hell didn't say shit."

Aer Lingus – "We didn't say shit on de radio. Oi would never say shit on de radio no matter if I taut it was shit or even felt loike it was shit or even, in fact, if it was shit!"

And another aircraft holding for departure.

Aircraft - "I'm f.....g bored."

ATC – "Who has just sworn on the R/T?"

Voice – "I said I was f.....g bored, not f.....g stupid!"

"Bournemouth, Bournemouth, Mayday, Mayday, Mayday, this is G-APRT, it's ok, I'm still in the air but I'm lost!"

ATC – G-APRT, Bournemouth, what was your last known position?"

G-ARPT – "When I was number one for take-off."

"Air China 221, turn left heading 230 degrees."

"Loger, Air China 221, turning lite heading 230 degrees."

"Negative. Air China 221, turn LEFT heading 230 degrees."

"Air China 221, turning reft lite heading 230 degrees."

"Air China 221, I say again, TURN LEFT, right?" – Doh!

And then,

"Speedbird Concorde, can you descend twenty thousand feet in the next eighteen miles?"

A rather refined voice answers, "I daresay I could, old boy, but I couldn't bring the aircraft with me."

"Red 2, am I contrailing?"

"No."

"Oh, in that case, you're on fire!"

"London, good afternoon, we're hand-flying today as the autopilot is not functioning properly." Another calls straight afterwards, "London, good afternoon, we're on autopilot as the crew isn't functioning properly!"

"Manchester, was that direct Honiley or Holly?"

"Direct Honiley, that's H-O-N-I-L-E-Y, I don't know a Holly."

Another voice says, "Oh I do!"

# Air Traffic Controllers can be quick too!

Pilots always want to fly the shortest route possible. Figures – saves fuel, saves time, saves having to work out too many headings! They can get very shirty if they are driven by us in ATC out of their way for any reason, even though they have no idea what that may be. So, it's basically straight line or big complaint.

As an example, try this. A propeller-driven airliner (and therefore slower than others) is inbound to Amsterdam and has to be given extended routings to fit in with the others who are faster. After a fair bit of being driven around the sky, the Captain is not at all happy and says so to the controller.

"Can we hurry this up? I'm seeing parts of Holland I've never seen before."

ATC replies, "If you don't shut up, you'll be seeing parts of Germany you've never seen before!"

Italy next.

ATC – "Woulda you alika the Milano weather?"

"Yes please, and we are ready to copy."

ATC – "Ah sorry, we don'ta have the Milano weather at thee momenta bit don'ta worry, eesa alwaysa gooda."

A military airfield at around midnight. An out-of-the-blue call from one of their aircraft based there returning from a sortie.

"Guess who!"

The controller pulls himself away from the book he was reading, heads to the lighting panel and turns off the airfield lights. And then says to the aeroplane, "Guess where!"

I was on duty one gorgeous, cloudless afternoon when I recognised the pilot's voice in this next exchange as that of one of my fellow controllers at Bournemouth a couple of years previously and decided to have a laugh with him.

"Bournemouth, good afternoon, City Flyer 97C, Gatwick to Jersey, request the Bournemouth weather."

He didn't really need the weather; he just fancied a chat.

ATC (me) – "City Flyer 97C, I'll give you the weather shortly, but before I do give you the weather, let me say that it's much, much better weather here than it ever was under any Labour government!"

"Ah, thanks very much," he said and didn't stay for the weather anyway. Must have known it was me!

# Cabin Crew get in on the act of being clever

Piers Brosnan is probably most famous as an actor for his role as James Bond. He flew quite a lot with BA during those days, having many important meetings across the Atlantic. On one particular night, he was flying back home. (Most eastbound aircraft crossing the Atlantic fly at night. Conversely, most westbounds fly in daylight, taking advantage of the time difference. That is why Concorde could depart London after breakfast and arrive in New York in time for second breakfast, as any Hobbit could tell you.). Anyway, as Piers settled down for a sleep, he asked that one of the crew wake him well before landing as he wanted to look fresh for any photographers lurking in the terminal. Fair enough, as we wouldn't want James Bond looking dishevelled and red-eyed now, would we? He made it quite clear that he should be roused well in advance. About two hours or so from London, one of the crew went to wake him. After a few shakes, he was still asleep and was left that way as the crew were becoming busy with the breakfast service. On waking, he was very annoyed and called the crew to complain.

"I told you I needed to be woken *well* in advance of the landing, and you didn't," he complained.

Quick as a flash, she replied, "Well sir, you were shaken but never stirred!"

He thought that was very clever and had a good laugh about it.

Picture the scene – a westbound transatlantic flight. On board was this enormous American woman who was dressed loudly and talked just the same. She complained about just about everything, from the size of the bag of peanuts to the bright sunlight streaming through her window to the tardy delivery of her gin and tonic. After lunch had been served and the coffee was on its way, she interrupted one of the crew and asked him, "Excuse me young man, but can you tell me, what's an *oot*?"

"I beg your pardon madam, a what?"

"An *oot*."

"I'm sorry madam, I don't have any idea what an *oot* is. Why do you ask?"

"Well, I never drink or eat anything animal unless I know what the animal is."

"I'm sorry, madam, I still don't have a clue what it is you're asking me."

"It says on the bottom of this milk carton 'contains *oot* milk.'"

The long-suffering crew member had a look at the carton and it did, indeed, state that it contained *oot* milk, but *oot* was spelt UHT!

"Oh, that's an Upper Hiberian Tushy, Madam. Absolutely lovely."

"Sounds delicious," she said, settling back into her seat.

How he contained his laughter is a credit to him and his training.

I got on board a Brymon Airways flight from Southampton to Newcastle one morning, and the cabin crew director told me that she would be making all the flight announcements using the titles of ABBA songs; everyone I got right would earn me a gin and tonic. I listened very carefully and it went something like this. (I've edited it a bit to save you from being bored, as you usually are during cabin safety announcements. Aren't you? Yes, thought so.)

Before we were airborne –

"Good morning, ladies and gentlemen, and welcome aboard this Brymon Airways Dash8 flight to Newcastle. Your lifejacket is under your seat. In the event of a landing on water, remove the jacket from its container, pass it over your head and tie in a double bow on the left. Do not inflate the jacket until you are outside the aircraft. There is a WATERLOO on this aircraft at the front of the cabin on the right-hand side. Please fasten your safety belt and make sure your table is stowed."

Then, just as we levelled into the cruise –

"If there's a Mr Dan Singqueen on board today, please make yourself known to the cabin crew. That's Mr Dan Singqueen."

And then the flight crew got involved –

"Good morning, ladies and gentlemen, this is the First Officer speaking. We are at our cruising level of 19000ft and the flight should be smooth, but Mamma Mia, the weather in Newcastle is very cloudy and quite windy so don't Take a Chance, take a raincoat. We hope you're enjoying this short flight with us today."

And just after we landed –

"Ladies and gentlemen, Knowing Me Knowing You, you'll realise that we've landed in Newcastle. We hope you have a pleasant onward journey. From all the crew, goodbye."

To finish, you know the way the crew put on music as the aeroplane pulls up to the gate? Well, I heard a bloke say to the stewardess as he was leaving the aircraft, "Thank You for the Music!"

Always listen very carefully to every cabin announcement – I got five gin and tonics!

# The tricks people play

Southampton airport's departure lounge has enormous windows which look out onto the apron where the aircraft are parked. You can watch the aeroplanes come and go and even see the flight deck crew as they pull onto the gate. One day, whilst waiting for my flight, I saw the Dash8 of Brymon Airways pulling onto the gate and recognised the Captain, a good friend of mine, and he spotted me. After meeting the passengers and shepherding them into the arrivals area, the ground crew were passing and I asked them if they would kindly ask the Captain whether I could travel on the flight deck as I was an air traffic controller at Newcastle and my standby situation looked dubious. One of them obliged and went out to the aircraft. A short conversation ensued, after which, on her return, she told me that the Captain had said that the flight deck jump seat wasn't available. I said that it was vital that I travelled today as I had their landing clearance at Newcastle in my pocket! She went back to the aircraft and created much laughter and shaking of fists when she told them what I'd said. "Children!" was the look she gave me when she got back inside the terminal building.

On another flight, I was sitting opposite David Gower. He didn't say a word the whole flight, he hardly ever looked up, and he definitely didn't smile when the announcement on landing was, "They think it's all over – it is now."

I've got two stories here of flight deck crew being very childish and upsetting one or two of the new cabin crew on their first flights with the airline. The first victim saw the funny side, the second not so much.

She had passed her course with flying colours and was assigned her first flight. She met the crew and was introduced to the Captain, who asked her a few questions about her training course and then about some of the equipment on board and where it was located. He was quite satisfied with her answers, so off they went to board the aircraft, she chatting nervously to the others.

The take-off and climb went smoothly and when they got to the cruising level, the Captain called her into the flight deck.

"We've got a hydraulic problem, so I need you to flush the rear starboard toilet every five minutes to get us safely to Palma," said the Captain. Unbeknown to her, the rest of the cabin crew were in on the ruse. So, every five minutes for the rest of the flight, which lasted a further two hours, she studiously flushed the rear starboard toilet a total of twenty-four times!

After the turn round and with the passengers just about to board for the journey home, she politely asked the Captain whether the hydraulic problem had been fixed.

"What hydraulic problem?" he said.

I don't think she spoke to any of the crew all the way home.

The second story may upset you a bit, but don't take it too seriously. Unfortunately, the poor victim reported the crew and they enjoyed a visit to the Chief Pilot's office without the tea and biscuits!

Here's the setup. The First Officer obtains a sick bag and half fills it with milk and crushed digestive biscuits. He pops the bag down beside his right leg and out of sight. About an hour or so into the flight, it got a bit bumpy so the Captain bing-bongs the Cabin Service Director and asks him if the newbie could bring a sick bag for the First Officer as he "wasn't feeling too well". The newbie arrives and hands the bag to the First Officer, who pretends to be sick into the bag, in the process exchanging the empty bag for the one by his leg. He's handing the bag back to the newbie when the Captain reaches for it saying, "Give me that, I haven't had my breakfast yet," and proceeds to drink from the bag. At this point, the newbie fainted and had to be revived later. Airline Captains – 'orrible aren't they?

Flight crew 2 v Cabin crew nil, but they score a good one now.

On a very busy flight from London to Amsterdam, the cabin crew were extremely busy serving drinks, lunch and duty-free sales. The flight crew were aware of this but kept on and on demanding their duty-free cigarettes, which they were allowed (this in the days when smoking was permitted on airliners).

It was pointed out to the flight crew that the cabin was extremely busy on this short flight, but no matter, the demands went on and on. Now, from the start of the descent, it takes roughly half an hour to get on the ground, and the cabin crew can be even busier during this period as they get everything cleared away and the cabin secured for landing. Suddenly, the flight deck door was opened and the pilots heard a shout from one of the cabin crew. "FAGS!" she yelled and fired six packets into the flight deck, slamming the door on leaving. This was a bit startling but they deserved it.

The interesting bit is that she had opened each packet and removed a couple of cigarettes from each one. This meant that they were very loose inside the packets and when they hit the instrument panel, they all fell out! Cigarettes all over the flight deck – that'll teach them!

# What's it got to do with you, big nose?

*Concorde Standard Woodley Arrival*

The supersonic era was ushered in one special day in 1976 and ushered out one sad day in 2003. Concorde – what a machine, what an inspiration, what an achievement. Designed in the 50s, she had a clockwork cockpit (try saying that after a glass or two). No fancy magenta line for her, no digital anything apart from the Captain's finger, no iPad screen to keep everything in the one place. Just truly magnificent row after row of clock-like instruments. The pilot needed eyes in the back of his eyes to spot any discrepancy in the myriad readings, but they were big, fairly easy to read and all in your face. No hidden bits as on some 737s.

She needed two pilots and a flight engineer to take care of the four huge frigate engines that powered her and all the onboard systems; two pilots would never have been enough. Never got the chance to fly on Concorde but cleared it for take-off and landing many times at Heathrow. Just another aircraft to us but the only one we could hear on departure as she usually used a full after-burner for take-off. Magnificent.

As time went by, we and the crews got used to handling this fabulous aircraft. She was no trouble when on the ground or departing but a bit of a handful on the approach. This was because she needed to fly slightly faster than the others – say 250kts downwind instead of 210 and 190 on final approach, with everyone else doing 160. She could easily catch the one ahead if we weren't careful. Accurate and canny radar vectoring usually solved any problem, but it took a while to get used to the differing speeds.

Flying any approach is demanding on the flight crew, so one of Concorde's First Officers came up with the idea that the various speeds required on the approach, and when to reduce them, along with the points of turning the aircraft, could be programmed into the onboard computer and be flown by the autopilot without any hands-on flying by the crew. This, they reckoned, would save substantial amounts of fuel as the power settings would also be automatic. Nice idea, for which he was paid handsomely, no doubt. And so Concorde, coming in from New York one evening, asked Heathrow Approach for a standard Woodley – Ockham arrival for runway 28L. We had been briefed regarding Concorde's fully automatic approach and had been instructed to offer the approach as much as possible, taking into account other traffic. As luck would have it, we weren't too busy at that moment, so we cleared Concorde for the approach and sat back to watch. She flew the approach without incident, but after the landing, we looked at each other in the Approach control room with much shrugging of shoulders and scratching of heads. "What the hell was so special about that?" we thought. We could've got him on the ground a lot quicker!

The next day, "Heathrow Approach, Speedbird (company callsign of BA) Concorde 002, request a standard Woodley – Ockham arrival for 28L."

"Speedbird 002 Heathrow, would you like the standard approach or would you prefer a more expeditious one?" (Ie, a shorter route and therefore faster.)

Deathly hush for maybe fifteen seconds whilst he pondered this.

"Roger Heathrow, we'd like a more expeditious approach."

So we vector Concorde from roughly the Reading area onto the final approach over London using the radar. Our first action is to route the aircraft direct to a point SE of Heathrow before any turn to final approach. This action takes him way inside his automatic track and shortens the total route by around seven or eight miles. We turn him onto the base leg at least five miles before the automatics would have done, therefore reducing by quite a bit his actual distance flown. We also reduce his speed much later than the standard approach, which means he can keep the aircraft "cleaner" (less drag and therefore less fuel) for longer, with the power at a low setting.

No comments were made by the pilot about the approach at the time. However, later that evening, we got a phone call from the Captain to say that we had just saved him a ton of fuel – he didn't mean a lot of fuel, he meant a *ton!* That, for two Concordes a day landing at Heathrow, added up very quickly to quite a substantial sum of money. So, in the days to follow, Concorde, instead of asking for a standard Woodley – Ockham arrival, shortened it to, "We'll take a hand job for 28L!"

What a feather in our cap. It paid off too for quite a few of us as we were awarded free flights to Washington and back on Concorde. Sadly, I had left Heathrow before my trip was awarded. Boohoo. ("You stupid boy!")

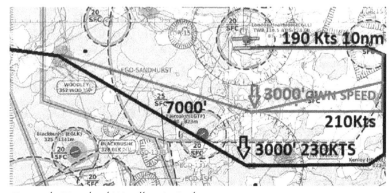

*Concorde Standard Woodley Arrival*

# ALLO, ALLO

Whenever we have a change of Prime Minister, there's no hootin' and hollerin'. It's all usually done quietly and with dignity. Compare that with the arrival of a new American President, for example.

At Heathrow, there is a VIP suite where special people are met on arrival or despatched from when leaving the UK. They are looked after with the red carpet treatment (and the rest!). Heads of State, Presidents, the Royal Family are all routed through this special place in the airport. This is where the Queen embarks and disembarks, and she does so without any pomp or ceremony. All quietly and discreetly done. You'd hardly know she was there, just like the President of the United States – yeh, right!

What a palaver we had to endure for Ronnie Reagan's arrival. Security guards all over the place, including in the air and inside the control tower. Shifty looking individuals in dark, shiny suits, talking up their sleeves and lurking about in the tower whilst we quietly got on with our work moving the aeroplanes around. They had earpieces in their ears and were constantly talking. This was a distraction to us, but we just had to live with it for the duration until Uncle Ronnie had either left the VIP suite en route to the Palace or departed in his private 747, Air Force One. Then they would suddenly and silently disappear.

The really funny bit of all this nonsense still makes me laugh, especially as they were all very stern and never smiled. The earpieces they wore were connected to their ears by a curly white cable which stood out starkly and obviously from their dark clothing – unmissable and hardly secretive. But the *really* funny bit was their callsign. When they called their counterparts in the VIP suite, the callsign they used was "Nighthawk". What a laugh, and we did that a lot!

"Allo, Allo, this is Nighthawk calling, Nighthawk calling" – they never actually said that, but we silently did every time we heard them use the callsign up their sleeve. Laugh? We nearly cried, and they never knew why, remaining stern and stoically upright, which made it all the funnier!

Talking about the sitcom itself, I had the privilege of meeting the actor, Arthur Bostrom, who played the French policeman in the series. I had just watched a live performance at the Pier Theatre in Bournemouth and was having a drink in the Pier bar when the cast came in. He was very interested when I told him he was famous in British aviation circles but was bemused as to how. So, I explained.

Every morning, *every* British aircraft routing down through France to say, Palma or Tenerife, on being handed over to France control said,

"France control, good moaning, this is Danair........................"

"France control, good moaning, this is Monarch......................."

"France control, good moaning, this is Britannia........................"

Every morning, every aeroplane. Can you imagine how the French controllers felt? *Every* morning, *every* aeroplane, over and over and over!

Arthur was most impressed and said, "Thunk you very mooch for tacking the tribble to peese on theese massage."

# Dunsfold

You've heard already how I was so foolish as to attempt a change in my career from aviation to show biz. What an eejit, but it at least gave me the chance to a) try something different and b) still work in aviation, even on a part-time basis, to keep my hard-fought licence alive. Here's where I got that chance.

The best things in life are flukes, I've discovered. Having left Heathrow and started my radio "career", I wrote to British Aerospace at Dunsfold Aerodrome asking whether they had a position for a part-time ATCO. I got a phone call by return from the SATCO asking how did I know. "Know what?" I asked. "How did you know one of our controllers will shortly be going on maternity leave?" Bingo!

Test pilots are crazy people! A necessary quality as they are the ones who put our airliners through their paces before a CofA (glossary) can be issued. And boy, do they put them through it. They put aircraft into places, positions and altitudes that aeroplanes can't go just to see how far they can be pushed. Airline pilots would never do the things test pilots do, thank God! Military test pilots are even crazier, as I found out. However, one thing they are is extremely good at their job.

Dunsfold, about 7 miles west of Gatwick, was owned by British Aerospace. Nowadays, you might see it on the TV programme Top Gear. At times, the control tower and a few aeroplanes, including a Boeing 747, can be seen flashing past as cars speed around the airfield. It was where the Harrier Jump Jet and the Hawk aircraft (Red Arrows) were built and test flown by a small group of military test pilots, the most famous of whom was John Farley. He developed the Farley take-off in a Harrier, whereby he would put the aircraft into a hover at about 100 feet, then, using the Reaction Controls, put the aircraft into a 60-degree nose-high attitude using the engine nozzles to suit so that it was still hovering. He would then apply maximum power and simply rocket-climb away! The Harrier had only one engine, so an engine failure would have killed him and the aircraft outright. He practised this at Dunsfold, and it was quite a sight, I can tell you! A Harrier climbing virtually vertically from behind trees – wow!

Each pilot had his own callsign, usually the first letter of his surname. Hawker 69 was the exception to the rule. This was the callsign of Taylor Scott, who was tragically killed during a test flight in a Harrier. You may remember the tale of an empty Harrier being intercepted by jet fighters over the Atlantic. That was Taylor's aeroplane from which he had been pulled, we think, as he was checking the oxygen supply. The aircraft flew well out over the Atlantic until it ran out of fuel and crashed into the waves. A tragic loss of an excellent pilot and a bloody good bloke. It was a very sad day at Dunsfold the day after the tragedy.

Hawker "R" was Chris Roberts. When I had moved from Dunsfold to Bournemouth, he called me one day on a low-level route from St. Catherine's Point on the Isle of Wight via the Needles and Hengistbury Head to Wimborne in a Hunter aircraft.

I said, "Morning Chris," but he didn't recognise my voice. Probably too busy.

Hawker "T" was Graham Tomlinson. There were two hover pads, one at each end of the runway, which were used by Harriers. Graham was doing hover trials at the easterly pad when he asked me whether the RAT (see glossary) was deployed. I told him to hold on whilst I found the binoculars. "Never mind, I'll come across to you." The noise as a Harrier hovered right outside the tower windows was earth-shattering! Wish I'd had my camera.

Hawker "F" was Swiss, Heinz Frick. He was Chief Test Pilot in my day and an absolute genius when it came to test flying, if a bit insane! He actually dead-sticked a Harrier onto Boscombe Down near Salisbury one Christmas Eve after the aircraft suffered an engine failure. If you're ever in a Harrier and its engine fails, do *not* try this. Bail out! A Harrier with no engine flies like a brick.

One afternoon, just after I had been validated in the tower at Dunsfold, Hawker "F" was returning from a sortie in a Harrier with a jammed stabiliser. This made the aeroplane extremely difficult to control, so a Full Emergency was initiated by yours truly for his arrival. Everyone was ready as the aircraft approached the runway. He was cleared to land, but what happened next came as a complete surprise to me and the airfield fire and rescue service. We all expected him to land and end up in a heap in the barrier at the far end of the runway. But he suddenly announced that he thought that he could fix the problem, so he went around from the approach and flew out over the south coast! After a short while, he had indeed solved the problem and returned to Dunsfold to make an ordinary landing, so saving his own life and that of the Harrier!

A notable trial we did at Dunsfold was trying out the red, white and blue Red Arrow smoke colours using a new blend of fuels. What a laugh! Engineers fitted a Hawk with the equipment and got it airborne, and then we advised the engineers how the smoke looked. The first run gave us Pink, White and Blue. The second run Pink, White and Black! The third Pink, Pinkish and Black! It took all day and a selection of flights to get the colours right, but they managed in the end. Just as well, as you can imagine the announcement at the next airshow: "Ladies and gentlemen, please welcome the aerobatic team of the RAF, the Pinkish Arrows!"

There were other pilots at Dunsfold, including Dave, who flew the company Jetstream runabout between other BAE airfields in the UK. He was yet another great pilot but nowhere near as crazy as those I've mentioned! Happy days and a privilege for me to work with some consummate professionals.

I was also able to do some physical training at Dunsfold for the London Marathon, which I ran in 1987. The flying stopped each day at 5 pm, which meant I had the airfield all to myself. Flat ground, plenty of alternative routes, nobody else about. I bet *you* can't boast that you've run along an airport runway!

# More special people
# that I know

We've heard already about two aviator friends (Pilot Brian and Controller Kevin), as well as the test pilots at Dunsfold, but there are a few more I'd like to mention, so please indulge me for a moment or two. I'll mention some pilots first.

Between 1997 and 2001, I was working at Newcastle Airport, but my home is on the south coast and I was commuting with Brymon Airways between Newcastle and Southampton virtually every week. I got to know most of the Brymon pilots, and I am eternally grateful to them for allowing me access to their "office" on a regular basis.

I learnt more about aviation in those four years than in the previous twenty-five!

We enjoyed some really technical conversations and discussed some fascinating subjects that only experienced colleagues can understand.

Peter Lucas – Chief Base pilot of Brymon Airways at Newcastle. A consummate professional and always keen for me to be in the flight deck jump seat. Very friendly and always just as keen to learn about ATC as I was to learn about piloting aeroplanes. We were just airborne from Southampton one poor-weather morning. I watched a person totally at ease in his environment as we climbed into the cloud, with Peter hand-flying the Dash8. Smooth as silk, we levelled at 2500ft in moderate turbulence, power back just enough and nicely trimmed, he with a big smile on his face. A delight to observe, and I felt very safe in his hands.

Andy Duffil – Brymon Airways. Another excellent pilot and a nice guy to boot.

To close the throttles at the top of the descent and not touch them again until you're on the runway takes a *lot* of good judgement, a lack of other traffic to get in the way and a good flight deck team. You need to be at the correct speeds to be able to select the flaps and undercarriage at the right altitudes, with the aeroplane at the right altitude for landing and the checks complete. The mental arithmetic gymnastics required are considerable. To be able to adjust the height versus the speed versus the rate of descent required to get the height off in time from any particular distance from touchdown is exactly what Andy did on one approach into Southampton. Power off from FL100 thirty-five miles from touchdown doing 190kts initially. He judged the speed reductions perfectly at flap and gear-selection speeds, along with the descent rate, and greased it onto the runway – what a professional. Sadly, tragedy struck when Andy was killed shortly afterwards when teaching a teenager to fly. They were hit by another aeroplane doing aerobatics. A sad and unnecessary loss to us all.

Gary Morton – Brymon Airways, then Maersk. Gary is one of the most laid-back pilots I've ever been with and a really good flyer. Flying south from Newcastle at night in cloud with freezing conditions, I noticed a gentle vibration through the flight deck jump seat. I mentioned it to Gary, who couldn't feel it but switched on the landing lights so that he could see the leading edge of the port wing. Sure enough, we were accumulating a large build-up of ice. He ran the de-icing boots to bash the ice off and asked Pennine radar for a climb to a warmer level. We were held at the freezing level for quite some time and the vibrations were getting worse. After a while, he calmly said to Pennine, "How's it going with that level?" No drama. We were in cloud at night at 19000ft accumulating ice and he could've been on the phone to his mum! (I've another story later about another pilot in icing conditions who was just as calm.)

On another occasion, landing at Newcastle, in a stiff crosswind which he called a mere zephyr, we were caught by a dangerous windshear during the landing flare. Power on, stick forward a touch, then power off, stick back and we were on the runway with hardly a bounce. When I congratulated him on the smooth touchdown, he replied, "We almost died back there." *And* he was serious!

My sincere thanks to all the aircrew at Brymon Airways, including Simon Mason, Howard Bosworth, Richard Francis, Phil Rees, Derek Wright, Aidan Bell, Chris Laird, Jerry Clark, Giora, Simon (Rambo) Ramsey, Matt Redhead, Stuart Knowles, Chris Foster, Richard Carregate, Sid Fleet, Roger Elde (a Canadian, sounded just like Donald Sutherland!), Wally Rhodes and Eunice Hollis. And in the cabin were Heather, Jude and Helen. What a time I had.

Captain Hamilton – British Airways. Now, I've never met this pilot but I've been treated to his capabilities as a pilot who has passenger comfort number two on his list, second only to passenger safety.

The Boeing 757 is a fantastic aeroplane but it cannot take off by itself! However, once airborne, it could fly itself to its destination, land itself and stop on the runway. On departure, it needs a pilot to pull the controls back at the appropriate speed and get it climbing. No real mystery there but it's the way the controls were used by Captain Hamilton that impressed me. I even wrote to British Airways with my compliments, and they told me that he had hand-flown the aeroplane to the top of the climb that day. I've experienced nearly 750 take-offs, and this particular one sticks in my mind as a peach. Why? Well, the way in which he feathered off the pressure on the controls to bring the aircraft gently into the climb, and the levelling off twice on the way to the cruising level was just so gorgeous it was almost like flying on a feather bed or Aladdin's magic carpet. I was sitting down the back on this flight but could picture him thoroughly enjoying himself. If I hadn't written, I wondered whether he would ever have known that someone on board appreciated his talents. I doubt that it would have mattered, but I hope he was pleased anyway.

Nigel "the Perv" Pervis was an instructor in a small flying school at Bournemouth Airport, and I deeply hope his nickname was because of his surname and not his alleged personality! He was an excellent pilot instructor and well-liked by everyone in the flying school and the airport in general. Every time he landed back at Bournemouth after trips to his favourite Isle of Wight, as he taxied in, he would let his student control the plane whilst he opened the door, lean out standing up and give us a salute as he went by! Lovely bloke.

He was just airborne from Sandown on the Isle of Wight one afternoon when the engine failed and he landed in a tree! All four on board survived, but Nigel died shortly afterwards sitting in his chair watching the telly. Life's crazy, isn't it?

Now for some ATC colleagues.

Paul Wilson – "A" watch Heathrow. Heathrow Approach control back then (80s) had one controller working the north holding stacks of Bovingdon (nr St Albans) and Lambourne (Essex), with another working the south holding stacks of Ockham (nr Epsom) and Biggin Hill (at Biggin Hill!). There was also a controller to whom the other two handed traffic to be positioned onto the final approach four miles apart. To make things simpler and therefore safer, it was agreed that the No1 north controller was "in charge" of the overall flow. It was he or she who would decide which aircraft was following who, and this was accomplished with the north controller telling the south controller the decision over the intercom. With Paul on No1 south,

I as the controller in charge never, *ever* had to intercom him with the intended flow and he never *ever* had to ask me! We just instinctively knew, by simply looking at the overall radar picture, what the traffic order was to be.

A great colleague and easy to work with.

Mark Laws – Dunsfold. Same expertise as Paul except that he was in radar and I was qualified in aerodrome control only. Simply by monitoring each other's frequency, we knew what the other was thinking and what would be happening next. Granted, Dunsfold was a lot quieter than Heathrow, but the principle is the same.

An efficient and safe operation enhanced by anticipation and expertise.

Eddie Duncan – Belfast International. One of my first watch supervisors and a stickler for the rules. He used to ask me on every morning shift we worked together what the freezing level of the day was. I was very perplexed by this as I was a lowly aerodrome control trainee just starting out back then and knowledge of the freezing level is of little interest or importance to airport controllers. On asking another recently checked-out colleague why Eddie was always asking me what the freezing level of the day was, he said, "Oh, Eddie just wants to know whether you've studied the weather forecast."

Very subtle, but you know what? I knew the freezing level on every shift I've ever done – useless information, really, but a good habit formed.

Geoff Large – watch manager "A" watch Heathrow. My first boss and my second father. He and I just clicked when I arrived in 1977. He took me under his wing and taught me so much. He was always calm in a storm, took great pride and interest in what I was doing and monitored my progress to becoming a fully-fledged Heathrow controller very closely. When he retired in 1983, I lost a friend and a father figure and frankly lost my way in the world a bit. He died in February 2022 about a month or so before his 101st birthday! He had a great life in aviation, but, just like the rest of us, he couldn't go on for ever.

Colin Batchelor – watch manager Bournemouth 1976. I can't thank Colin enough for his warmth, his sense of humour and his professionalism. I was training in 1976 and was on his watch. He had suffered polio as a child and had a calliper on his leg. He had to sleep sitting up as a result of the illness, and he couldn't get up the stairs easily. But when he did manage the stairs, Colin used to sit in his supervisor's chair and laugh like a drain all day. Nothing ever brought him down, and he was a delight to be around. Many years later, when I was Deputy Senior controller at Bournemouth Airport, I used to remember him with extreme fondness and would emulate him as often as I could. He was married to a French girl, and after he retired, they moved to her village in France where he eventually became the mayor. I am not surprised. Be like Colin and laugh like a drain all day – what a wonderful philosophy for life.

Steve Weeks – fellow ATC instructor College of ATC, Bournemouth Airport. Steve is ex-military, having served with the RAF in the UK and Cyprus. He arrived at the College just after me and we hit it off straight away. We kept each other sane as we taught ab initio controllers their skills. At least, that's what I tried to do! What I mean is that the trainees just wanted to pass their exams, whereas I was hoping to ignite the fires of enthusiasm and an everlasting love of aeroplanes and aviation in general.

Sadly for me, this was a lost cause. Not many trainees in my nine years at the college showed much overall excitement for their careers. However, Steve understood much better than I just how a student's mind works and did his best to keep me "under control". A good office mate and a highly valued friend to this day.

Leo Murphy – my first OJTI instructor Belfast International airport. If there's one thing for which I will be eternally grateful to Leo, it's that he used to fall asleep at the soonest opportunity when he and I were on duty! There comes a time in every trainee's on-the-job training when he should be left alone to get on with it. If the instructor is always looking over the trainee's shoulder, the trainee risks losing his or her self-confidence to work independently. This is called in the trade a "long lead" and Leo was an expert in this. On purpose or not I'll never know, but it worked very quickly for me and allowed me to build the self-confidence necessary to become good enough to work at Heathrow for ten years. The "sleep-deprived" Murphy always said that there was nothing better than a good trainee!

Brendan McCartney – fellow "A" watch Heathrow controller. Now you've probably worked with people who, after a long day or difficult shift, run to their car to get home sharply. Brendan was no different except that he used to run *into* work as well, such was his enthusiasm for the job! I'd never seen anyone do that before, and I still never have. Always professional, always friendly, always up for a laugh and a delight to be on shift with. He was one of the training officers on the watch, and when I had difficulty applying the departure separations, he showed me how, by transmitting to every aircraft, when it was safe to do so, "Cleared for take-off." "There you are," he said. "If you don't say cleared for take-off, you'll never learn how to apply the separations, simple." What a great lesson in how to "get on with it". We used to look at each other in the middle of a busy session and say, "One day we'll get a proper job." Thank God it never happened!

Roger Kunert – lighting panel operator Heathrow. An airport at night is an awe-inspiring sight. Coloured lights everywhere, on the ground and in the air, all with a different meaning and application, for example, the lines of green lights which delineate the taxiway centrelines. At most smaller airports, the lights are simply switched on at night and off again in the morning. However, because Heathrow is so big, not only was it split into numbered blocks for easy reference but it also required a huge lighting panel and someone to operate it, basically because there were so many green lights that they had to be selected on/off so that the aircraft could "follow the greens" to wherever it was going on the airfield. This was achieved by the panel operator selecting/deselecting the red stop bars between each block number, allowing for a continuous line of green lights for the aircraft to follow. I'm not sure what the situation is these days as there are now three GMC controllers, whereas in my day there was only one. Back then, the lighting panel operator was an integral part of the ground control team and wore a headset which monitored the GMC frequency. This enabled him or her to hear the routing given by the controller to any aircraft and set up the route required.

Heathrow was *busy*. Too busy to allocate a "block number" taxi route but not so hard to deal with on a good, clear-weather day as we could see the route required and could easily monitor the aircraft's progress. Bad weather and/or darkness were different beasts altogether. To give an actual route to each aeroplane using block numbers was the required standard, impossible at times, and this is where an experienced and efficient lighting panel operator was invaluable. Not only did it help to reduce the controller's RT workload, but it also meant that the stop bars could be suppressed in an efficient manner as opposed to an aircraft approaching a stop bar and having to stop.

Roger did not have an ATC licence, nor was he allowed to transmit on the frequency, but he had an inherent ability to anticipate the controller's instructions and set up an efficient route for the aircraft. So good was he that I personally trusted him to set the route up as he wished by simply transmitting, "Follow the greens." He would intercom me if necessary to say what he'd done, but that was a very rare occurrence and seldom needed.

What an asset to ATC Heathrow as a whole and the GMC controller in particular.

He was the best at what he did.

John Kilfoy – I got to know John and his family pretty well as he flew from Bournemouth and his mum and dad were living close to the airport. (Ted flew lots of aeroplanes with BEA, as well as during WW2.) I didn't fly much with John, but if his sailing is anything to go by, his flying is exceptional. Let me explain.

It was New Year's Day and we were in Ted's yacht with John at the helm, sailing from Lymington on the south coast over to Yarmouth on the Isle of Wight to have a celebratory lunch. The weather was perfect and we had a lovely crossing – apart from a dozen Dutch minesweepers that were crossing our path. Power must give way to sail at sea, so strictly speaking we had right of way. The Dutch thought otherwise. John had to dodge about four of them. No problem whatsoever, easy. No panic, no distress, just calm navigation and boat handling.

He was flying with Jersey European when we met. He's now a Captain with Easy Jet, having flown many years in A300s and 320s with Monarch until they went bust in 2017. I had the privilege of flying with him only once, from Leeds to Belfast City via the Isle of Man back in 1995. He asked me a favour. He said, "If you can get this surly co-pilot I'm with today to laugh, I'll buy you dinner."

You know what, that Kilfoy bloke still owes me!

# Just look at what you're missing!

Next time you're at a window seat on board, put the book or newspaper away and look out the window – you'll be amazed at what you will see. Clouds, of course, but keep looking. Contrails, other aeroplanes, the ghosts of wartime airfields, falling rain, the ground far below, cars on the roads. A pretty good view, but the best views are from the flight deck. The pilots can see roughly 300 degrees horizontally and around 45 degrees up and 45 down. Fabulous and sadly not available for the lowly passenger anymore.

I've been privileged over the years, since I learnt to fly as part of my Air Traffic Controller training in 1974, to have seen some majestic and breathtaking things through the front windows of aeroplanes. The closest passengers get to seeing the view is when some airliners have a camera on the nose wheel so that you can see the runway from way out. You can practice your landing technique too! Here are a few of the wonders I've seen:

One winter evening departing Southampton for Belfast City Airport. The sun set as we were taxiing out to the runway. We were delayed a bit, but just after we were airborne and in the climb, the sun rose and then set again about halfway through the flight. Two sunsets and a sunrise in the space of thirty minutes!

December 1997 – beautiful lunchtime at 19000ft over the Pennines, which had a light dusting of snow on the top of each one. Looked like sugar-coated doughnuts.

August 1974 – 3000ft over the Lake District and on my own!

Not a cloud or a bump – what a stupendous day, showing off the glory of the great British countryside and utterly unforgettable.

June 1984 – in a British Midland DC9 Edinburgh – Heathrow. We flew along a rope cloud for about 150 miles! Actually, just above and beside it and a very rare thing.

November 2017 – taxiing out at Gatwick for Madeira. The Airbus 320 had been de-iced but the wing still looked as if it was covered in glaze ice – not good and potentially dangerous. However, I had watched as the aircraft was de-iced at the gate so wasn't too concerned. As we began the take-off roll, all the ice slid off the wing in one whole piece! Looked like a pane of glass shattering behind us.

September 1984 – Luton to Malaga aboard a Boeing 720 of Monarch airlines. Flat calm on departure without a cloud in the sky. Spotted lots of fog patches lying peacefully in the dips and gullies of the countryside, along with three hot air balloons suspended below us. What a beautiful sight first thing in the morning.

August 2012 – Belfast to Southampton in a Dash8, dodging around many thunderheads. It was just like swimming through a field of kelp.

January 2000 – Newcastle to Southampton. Pitch black – in cloud – no turbulence.

Landing lights on – snowing – just the hum of the engines. How peaceful that was.

November 1994 – Brisbane to Cairns in Australia. Flying along the coast towards Cairns, there was quite a lot of cloud, so the view of our arrival into Cairns was going to be dull with nothing to see. Suddenly a hole appeared in the cloud directly ahead and we could see the city, the hills in the distance, the sea. We simply flew through the hole and there was the airport. Was that meant to be, or what?

Same flight – Cairns to Ayers Rock. So Ayers Rock is big, you reckon? From the air, it looks just like a part of the surrounding land and is virtually invisible. Took me a while staring right at it to see it!

September 2017 – in the cabin on the approach to Venice. The 21st century all around me on board the A319, whilst on the ground, the 20th with concrete and tarmac on the left and the 17th with water and marble on the right!

February 2022 – the setting sun's rays shining up through a snowfield of altocumulus behind me as we descended through the cloud – magical and romantic.

.

# Why is my flight delayed?????

Antalya airport in Turkey. Checked in for a four-hour flight to Bournemouth to be told there was a three-hour delay. "You're ATC – what's the problem?" asked one of our group. I had no idea at the time, but we could have had a l-o-n-g conversation about why flights are delayed! I'll try and cover a few reasons here, but if you get bored because there are so many, skip this chapter and take this chance to have a beer (which is what you should do if your flight's delayed – not too many though, you don't want to be delayed further as they throw you off the aeroplane and search for your luggage, which is unable to go without you). And there's the first reason.

"Bigair regret to announce the delay of flight BIG1. This is due to the late arrival of the incoming aircraft." All fine and dandy, but what does it mean, exactly? Blimey, here we go then, embarking on what could be the longest chapter in this book! The incoming aircraft is late arriving because it departed late from the preceding airport. *But why?* Let's take a flight and find out.

## The aeroplane

Airliners are very high-tech and need a lot of looking after. Most maintenance is done at night when the aircraft can be taken out of service, even for a prolonged period if required. Most planes go through this maintenance on time, but the odd occasion can arise when the maintenance has not been completed or is delayed. This means that the aeroplane will not be ready for the first departure of the day. The first flight of any day needs to be away on time. If not, the delay caused usually leads to further delays during the day, and if subsequent legs of the journey are delayed in their own right, the overall delays can become considerable. So, the timing of the first departure is vital.

An airliner can still depart if not all of its equipment is serviceable. This is called the MEL or minimum equipment list. This list allows airlines to fly the aeroplane subject to certain specified conditions, with particular equipment unserviceable. The Captain will check the maintenance (tech) log and see whether any equipment is unserviceable.

If an item on the MEL is u/s, he may still be able to depart but to the next destination *only*. This is known as an ADD (see glossary). If the defect can be repaired at the next destination, the flight can go. If not, the aeroplane is stuck until the problem is repaired, and the flight is therefore delayed or maybe even cancelled.

Other main items/problems with the aeroplane that cause delays include:

- the brakes can't be released
- one of the seats can't be put into the fully upright position
- a seat belt is missing
- one of the doors won't close/lock
- the flight deck computers need to be rebooted
- one of the radios doesn't work
- the flight deck torch is missing (in case of full electrical failure, especially at night)
- a toilet is out of use/broken
- the onboard communication system between the cabin crew and flight deck becomes u/s.

This list is not exhaustive, so if you hear of any other aeroplane failures that have caused you delays, please get in touch.

## Ground operations – airline

Our aircraft had arrived at the gate on time from its previous flight, but there was a problem opening the door. It took around ten minutes before the door was opened, another fifteen to get everyone off and a further thirty while the aircraft was cleaned and tidied ready for us to board, which we couldn't do because the crew hadn't arrived yet. Alarm clock failed to ring, busy roads, security check, briefing for the flight took longer than anticipated? At least the catering arrived on time!

An airport is a very busy place. Even small airports with few passenger flights can be ultra-busy at flight departure times. As we've said, it's vital that the first flight of the day is away on time. Missing passengers/drunk passengers/dithering passengers are a menace to airlines trying to get airborne on time and can be very difficult to deal with. Most of us are punctual and ready to go, but then the cabin crew start a headcount and the trouble starts! The number of passengers on board must match the figure on the load sheet and passenger manifest or we're going nowhere. If the Captain decides we're going without them, then the culprits' baggage needs to be found and offloaded. More delay. Eventually we're all on board and the doors are set to "Automatic and crosschecked" or "Armed". (These are terms which mean that the evacuation slides are able to act roughly the same as airbags in a car, ready to deploy if an emergency occurs.) However, there we sit, silently wondering what's going on now! There could be a number of reasons for this, but the two I'll mention here are

A) the jetway which connects us to the airport is jammed and refuses to move or

B) the tug we need to push us back from the stand is not available. Every aircraft nosed into the airport stands needs a tug to push the aeroplane away from the terminal building. Tugs need to be booked, so if you're late, you've probably lost the tug to another aeroplane.

OK, the tug has arrived and we're on the move, backwards, onto the taxiway.

Now the next chance for a delay. The tug has a pin which is used to lock the towbar onto the nose wheel and can be a right bugger to get out when the pushback manoeuvre has been completed. Various noises of banging, swearing, bumping can be heard in the flight deck, even above the noise of the engines. Not this time though, the pin came out real easy, but in the meantime, another two aircraft have pushed off their stands in front of us and we're stuck until their pins have been prised loose, by which time, as it's a freezing morning and because of the delay so far, the Captain decides that the aeroplane needs to be de-iced again! Shouldn't take long but the engines are shut down just in case we run out of sufficient fuel and need to be refuelled.

On the move again, this time going forward, hooray! However... The next two reasons why your aeroplane may be delayed are true stories.

When taxiing past a stationary plane at a holding point of the runway at Heathrow, a jumbo steered slightly off the taxiway centreline and clipped the tail of the waiting aircraft with its port (left-hand) wingtip, knocking the rudder out of alignment. Back to the stand for both, and replacement aircraft had to be found. In the meantime, a DC8, backtracking the runway to turn at the end to line up for take-off, misjudged the turn and got stuck on the grass with his main undercarriage in the mud for two days! Where's Joe Patroni (fictional TWA engineer famous in the *Airport* series of films) when you need him?

## Ground operations – airport

We may be at the holding point for the runway and ready to go, but we're not out of the woods yet at this airport. There are still *loads* of chances of a delay. (Bet you didn't want to hear that, but there are.) Here are a few examples of how easily any delay can happen, even when it seems as if we're up, up and away.

I cleared an Alitalia for take-off early one morning at Heathrow and watched as it over-rotated (got to too steep an angle on lift-off) and scraped the tail of the aircraft along the runway, destroying nine runway centreline lights in the process – runway closed immediately. Two hours' delay for everyone.

We're in a queue of aeroplanes waiting to take off. Ours has a red tail and we're quite big, although a long way from the terminal building.

"Ladies and gentlemen, this is the Captain. The tower knows we are here, but he's busy with the blue planes at the moment."

Then, just as our turn comes, there's a delay whilst a flock of birds is moved off the runway. You've heard, no doubt, about the A320 which ditched into the Hudson River in New York because of a bird strike? Well, the Hudson is a long way from London where we are, but we don't want to end up in the Thames either! However, we in ATC have the ingrained philosophy of providing a safe, orderly and expeditious flow of air traffic. We'll just have to wait our turn until the controller can fit us in. How does he or she do that? Well, it looks as if we'll be here for a while, so I'll try and explain how the flow is maintained by the departure controller at Heathrow. Fasten your seat belt; it could be a bumpy ride!

OK, let's look at a departure flow using the time separations laid down and acknowledged as being safe. In my day, there were large holding bays at each runway which we could use to shuffle the aeroplanes into the safest and most expeditious departure order. There were six departure routes, depending on the direction of the aircraft's destination. For example, aircraft going to Belfast would be given a Daventry departure (DTY), which meant it would route to the north west of Heathrow. South easterly departures were routed via Dover (DVR) and others to the south west via Midhurst (MID) – simple. So far, that is!

These days, most aeroplanes at Heathrow are jets and fly at roughly the same speeds. Not so in my day. We had all sorts, from Concorde to big jets to propeller-driven aeroplanes, creating huge differences in speeds and rates of climb.

This meant that to keep them apart if they were flying on the same route, we had to be very careful that faster aeroplanes didn't catch the one ahead. We also had to be aware that a faster aircraft departing behind a slower one even on a different route could be a recipe for disaster. These items are important but aren't the only things to think about.

You might have heard of a departure slot time? This was introduced in the early 80s so that traffic wouldn't be so busy as to overload another sector of the arrival airport. The departure slot was calculated so that the aeroplane arrived at its destination at its arrival slot. This was not easy to achieve should the departure miss its departure slot, and there were many occasions that a quick adjustment to the slot time wasn't achievable. Two or three hours' delay for an aeroplane already at the runway wasn't rare back then. Each slot time has a buffer, so there was a little headroom for a shuffle at the holding bay. The first slot times we issued had a buffer of the actual time plus six minutes. This was changed to minus three plus three to give more flexibility. Then it became minus two to plus eight minutes. I believe nowadays it is minus five to plus ten, probably due to the increasing sophistication and distribution of radars, especially in Europe. Minus five to plus ten - easy!

There you have it then – the departure controller at Heathrow had to balance routes, aircraft performance and laid-down separations before any aeroplane was cleared for take-off. If you want to be a controller at Heathrow, learn your times tables, otherwise you'll delay everybody!

Right, we've covered all the possible methods of being delayed – no, we haven't! There's the weather to take into account. That's where aeroplanes live, after all, and it can cause delays at times. Airliners are very tough machines. They are able to withstand extreme weather conditions, but sometimes it's much wiser to avoid severe weather altogether.

I was checked in for a flight from Belfast to London. The aircraft allocated to the flight was a Trident – a well-built British airliner but with a very small rudder, so small in fact that it was unable to depart in the strong crosswind that Belfast had that day. The cross runway, which was virtually into the wind, was not available due to maintenance, so we were stuck on the ground for about two hours until the wind had decreased enough to allow us to depart safely.

Another problem is the temperature. Too hot and the aircraft performance is severely restricted. That's why most airports in the Middle East, such as Dubai and Abu Dhabi, are really busy at night time. Even light aircraft can be "grounded" until things cool down, and here's the proof.

It was a rare day in County Fermanagh, Northern Ireland. My family had very kindly bought me a flight in a seaplane in and over Lough Erne for my 60th. It was scheduled for 4 pm in July 2013. Normally Northern Ireland in July is pretty hot anyway, it being marching season and all, but the weather is never (can't say that again!) blisteringly hot. The hottest day I've ever experienced in Ireland was the 19th of July 2013, the very day that I was due to fly in the seaplane. At around 3 pm, I got a phone call from the flight company to say it was too hot to get airborne safely from the part of the lough where we were staying and would it be alright to postpone it until 6 pm? No problems, so we gathered on the pontoon to await the arrival of our highly anticipated seaplane. Six came and went; half six came and went. At a quarter to seven, they rang again to say it was still too warm and would it be ok to delay until 8 pm? In July in Northern Ireland, it doesn't get dark until around 11 pm, so there were still no problems. Apart from needing the loo, we were quite happy.

We were eventually airborne at a quarter past eight. Just shows you how high temperatures can play havoc with aeroplane schedules.

We've already talked about tailwinds. Remember Salzburg? So let's now turn our attention to thunderstorms and rain. Thunderstorms are to be avoided if at all possible. The vertical winds inside a Charlie Bravo are very strong, strong enough, in fact, to shake an aeroplane apart. There are hurricane research teams who actually fly into hurricanes and their attendant thunderstorms, but we'll leave them to it, I think.

Thunderstorms are to be avoided by airliners, and your flight crew will do everything possible to do just that. The most dangerous part of a thunderstorm is one which we can't see. Now you'd think that there is no way you couldn't see a towering thunderhead, and that's true. The bits I'm talking about are over the top of the cloud and below the cloud. The bit over the top we can virtually disregard as the top is so high in a fully developed thundercloud that we can't get over the top anyway. It's the bit underneath which is the nasty bit.

As the air spills from the bottom of the cloud, it can develop into a severe downdraught called a microburst, and it can get to such strength that an aeroplane trying to get through it will be smashed into the ground. There was a nasty accident in Dallas in the late nineties which was caused by this phenomenon, but we didn't know just how dangerous it was back then. The good news is we know now and flight crews know exactly how to deal with it. That should help you feel a bit better.

Rain isn't really a problem unless it's falling from a thunderstorm! It makes the runway wet, obviously, but when the runway becomes flooded, that's when problems develop. Aquaplaning in your car is startling enough; try it in a jumbo! Or better still, don't try it! Runways have striations which help the water drain away reasonably quickly, but a flooded runway is to be respected and coped with by employing extreme caution. Landing on a flooded runway is never to be recommended.

Rain doesn't affect the aircraft engines too often, though. Certainly, an engine can ingest so much water that its performance is inhibited, but believe it or not, jet engines can have their performance enhanced by injecting a mixture of fuel and water into the engine. It heats the engine up and cools it down at the same time to give it more power! How weird is that? Even if a deluge of rain gets into the engine, the pilot, or more usually these days, the onboard computers, can select auto-igniters or "bangers" as they are colloquially known which operate continually to keep the fuel lit whilst the deluge continues so there's virtually no risk of losing an engine in heavy rain just when you need it! Rain only causes real concern when it freezes and becomes ice. That's something you really *don't* want inside a jet engine.

Engine anti-ice systems are on board every aircraft and are used extensively in freezing weather. An Air Florida pilot didn't select the engine anti-ice protection for a departure from a snowy Washington airport and ended up in the Potomac River.

I suppose Florida doesn't get much ice, and he was in the habit of not selecting it. Even the checklist and the co-pilot couldn't save them.

Ice forming on the aeroplane needs to be removed before we fly. You may see cherry-pickers with blokes in heavy waterproof gear hosing down an aircraft with glycol to keep the aeroplane clear of ice. Paris's Charles de Gaulle airport has what looks like a car wash building through which you taxi the aircraft and the "wash" tunnel sprays the aircraft with the fluid. Ice on the wings really ruins the smooth airflow across the wing, which affects the wing's ability to lift the aircraft *big time*, so needs to be removed.

Ice on a runway can also cause delays, both to arrivals and departures. In icing conditions, sand can be used on the runways and taxiways as on a road, but it can damage aircraft engines and tyres so is rarely used. De-icing fluid such as urea (cows' piss – yep, cows' piss!) is the favourite. Some airports have under-runway heating – posh, eh?

Ice and rain can cause problems for aircraft, so how do we in ATC get information regarding the state of the runway that the pilots need? This is done by dividing the runway into three sections and describing the conditions of each third. The most important thing the pilot needs to know is how wet the runway is and how efficiently the brakes can be used. We call this the braking action, and it is accurately measured by an airport vehicle equipped with a wheel set diagonally to the straight-ahead position and sped along the runway at thirty mph. The friction developed by this wheel against the runway surface is calculated and passed to aircrew as GOOD / MEDIUM / POOR braking action, and the condition of the runway as DRY / WATER PATCHES / WET / STANDING WATER / FLOODED. As the braking action report is vital, we stop all aircraft movements to allow the vehicle to carry out its run uninhibited. At Heathrow, this can take the guts of fifteen minutes because of the length of the runway and the requirement for the vehicle to do the run along each side of the runway, ie twice. Even though the resulting delays can quickly build up, safety is king and speed has to wait. We're delayed again!

The biggest contribution to our being stuck at the airport is fog. At least it used to be. In the 50s and 60s, Heathrow was closed for days on end due to the fog mixing with the smoke from the city and becoming smog. With the very light winds associated with fog, it used to hang around forever. London skies have been cleaned up a lot since then, and smog is no longer an issue. Fog still is, though, and any airport can be affected by it. However, technology has been ferocious in its advances, and we now have equipment on the ground and in the air which mitigates the worst effects of fog on operations. I said the worst effects as fog can still delay us, not so much for departures but for arrivals, which subsequently produce big delays for passengers on the return flight.

OK, we've survived all the possible delay situations at our departure airport and are now on our way at last. Beautiful day for flying, especially with a large gin and tonic and a good movie! We got away within an hour of our scheduled time, which, for me at least, is on time. We've got a healthy tailwind and are charging along. I visited Toronto in 2006 and had a two-hour delay for the return flight. However, we arrived in Gatwick on time as we had a scorching tailwind plum in the centre of the jetstream, which the crew had cleverly got us into. Eight hours Gatwick-Toronto and only six coming back. Sometimes "We regret to announce a delay due to the late arrival of the incoming aircraft" is irrelevant. It's also an easy excuse! (I never said that, OK?) Another easy excuse was to blame Air Traffic Control. This is not so valid these days as we've done a colossal amount of work internationally to reduce delays.

Anyway, you've heard of RVR (Runway Visual Range) in another chapter when we got back to Bournemouth from Dinard and how, even though the figure of 1000 metres RVR sounded quite a lot, in reality, it is still very poor viz and a hazard to landing traffic. Well, here's our next chance to be delayed.

The weather at our destination has fallen below our limits, so the crew can't even commence the approach. It's therefore necessary for us to go into a holding pattern until the fog lifts sufficiently. In the days when the ILS was first introduced, the limits permitted for airliners to attempt an approach were quite high. Nowadays, there might be no limit at all. Yep, zero visibility is acceptable under certain strict conditions. The major problem with zero viz is that when we get on the ground, how the hell do we get to the stand? Ground radar has solved many of those problems, but the aeroplanes need to move much more slowly, even so. Another problem is that the gap between each landing aircraft needs to be a lot wider, and I mean a *lot*, to keep it safe. The lander won't be able to taxi quickly off the runway, and he won't be able to see the taxiway easily so may be blocking the runway without our knowledge because we can't see him. (Ground radar has helped a lot to solve that problem too.) The next aircraft on the approach needs the ground equipment area of operation known as the Critical Area to be protected so that the aeroplane doesn't get any false indications from the ground equipment. The usual gap at Heathrow in clear weather is two and a half miles, but the runway and the Critical Area need to be sterile when the lander gets to four miles from touchdown, so you can see how fog slows everything down. Again, safety before expedition.

Right, we've arrived safely and are now joining the long wait for the baggage.

An exception to this rule was when I checked in at Las Vegas for a flight to Fort Lauderdale in Florida via Los Angeles and Atlanta. We had to change aircraft twice during the journey so it took a while. However, as we came down the stairs to baggage reclaim at Fort Lauderdale, we were met with our luggage going round and round on the carousel. It had got there before us!

Meanwhile, our aeroplane has "gone tech" which means it's got an equipment problem which can't be solved quickly and probably needs a spare part to be flown in. And so the departure delays start all over again!

Have we done it yet? Got to the end of this chapter? No chance!

Air Traffic Controllers have restricted hours which they are permitted to work to avoid fatigue. Airline crews have restricted hours they can work, or even be on duty, to avoid fatigue. Your aircraft may be delayed because of a medical emergency on the inbound flight. I was delayed at Gatwick for ten hours once because a woman on the inbound flight from Jamaica was smuggling condoms full of cocaine in her stomach and they burst! The aeroplane was diverted to New York and the crew then went "out of hours".

We once had a fire in the tower at Heathrow, which meant we had to go to the emergency tower, which was on top of one of the terminal buildings. It took a while to get there and get set up, and then we could use only one of the runways for everybody as we couldn't see the other one from where we were. Everyone suffered big delays for twenty-four hours.

Back in the early 80s, Heathrow decided to construct a new radar tower just beside the then staff car park adjacent to the tunnel. On top was to be a brand new, twin-channel radar and an enormous radar head. You might have seen it on your trips to and from Heathrow – it was unmissable. Anyway, this giant was supposed to be failsafe in the sense that it had two channels. One fails, the other clicks in straight away. Magic. On the first day of its operation, the turning gear failed and the big dish came to a stop! The magic suddenly disappeared under a cloak of embarrassed engineers and a huge roar of laughter from us. (Titanic couldn't sink either, eh!) Luckily we had other radars, so the aeroplanes suffered no delays.

In September 2017, I was returning from Venice to Gatwick. The flight was delayed but nobody told us! We checked in as normal and proceeded to security where the queue was roughly the equivalent of up and down the M1 and round the M25 – well, not really, but it felt like it! A bit of panic ensued as the departure time was looming.

We needn't have worried though because we arrived at the departure gate eventually, expecting to see it deserted, but it was packed. Only then were we told that there would be a delay. Phew! It gets better, though!

We were bussed out to the aircraft after about an hour and were all settled on board when the Captain told us there would be a further delay. (Heaven in Europe is where the Swiss organise everything – hell in Europe is where the Italians organise everything!) The baggage from the arrival flight hadn't even been unloaded at that point, and it took a further hour and a half for it to be taken off and ours to be loaded on. Venice Airport is way too busy for its size, so stay calm and delay on!

Just to finish off this chapter, remember back at the start, my delay out of Antalya coming back to Bournemouth? Three hours. Well, it wasn't until we got on board the aircraft for the return journey that we got the full explanation of why we'd been delayed for so l-o-n-g. It could've been a lot longer as the aeroplane came in from Manchester to pick us up and the crew had been on standby duty. The reason that it wasn't the usual Bournemouth aircraft and crew was that the aeroplane that morning had flown from Bournemouth to Palma in Majorca and had gone tech. It was stuck in Palma for two days.

Delays are difficult to predict, they can be sudden and the reasons are numerous. I've covered a few, but I'm sure there are hundreds more, so sit back, relax and enjoy the delay with us.

# AER LINGUS –
## the national airline of Ireland

We used to say that British Airways operate the Boeing 737 and Aer Lingus fly it.

Here is a true story which proves it.

ATCOs employed by National Air Traffic Services were expected to take two familiarisation flights a year and in our own time. Every year on my birthday, I would treat myself to a fam flight with Aer Lingus. I got to know a few of the Captains – Ted McCourt, Jim Dovey and the Captain of the flight that was hijacked on the approach to Heathrow, Eddie Foyle. I flew with Eddie on a return trip to Shannon from Heathrow in 1985, and we talked about that day during the flight. I told him how the word "Hijack" had come up on our radar and how we looked at each other wondering, "Is that correct?" We went through our procedures and realised that he *was* being hijacked. Eventually, he was diverted to Le Touquet on the French coast where the hijacker was overpowered and killed by the French police. Eddie was not at all impressed and was quite angry that they had stormed his aircraft without his permission and had killed the hijacker, whom Eddie was convinced had been talked out of his actions. Apparently, he was a priest who had gone doolally and had simply soaked himself in lighter fuel to seem serious. Very sad.

So, we got airborne and climbed in a big blue sky to our cruising altitude of 30,000ft.

Just before we crossed the Irish coast, we were transferred to Irish ATC. As soon as communication was established, Eddie said to his

First Officer, "Tell them we can see Shannon." Roughly one hundred and forty miles away and he could see Shannon Airport? No, he couldn't, but he knew where it was! We were transferred to Shannon tower but we didn't call them. What he did next was a thrill. He pushed his seat back, disengaged the auto-pilot, and descended to 3000ft. And then we flew around farms, over trees, along rivers and roads as if we were having a day out in a light aircraft. What a joy on a lovely day!

The trip back was also eventful and again a delight. At Shannon, we were told to follow a BA Trident to the runway. The Trident entered the runway at the mid-point position and turned left to backtrack for take-off, at which time Eddie said to the tower, "We can take it from here." We were cleared for take-off, entered the runway turning right and off we went, leaving the BA aeroplane in our wake! And there's more stitch-up of BA to come! Later, as we were descending into Heathrow, we heard Concorde call on the frequency. He was probably behind us but going a lot faster and would beat us into Heathrow. There was an easterly wind, so Heathrow was landing on runway 10L and we were planning for a straight-in approach.

Eddie casually but ever so cunningly increased the engine power, which kept us just ahead of Concorde. We got the straight-in approach to 10L we were hoping for. Meanwhile, Concorde had to go all the way to the Ockham holding stack and all the way back to the Woodley area for his approach! Neatly done, Eddie.

On another fam flight with Aer Lingus, further proof that they flew the 737 was afforded to me. This is one for the specialists, so forgive me if I get a bit carried away. See if you can follow it, anyway.

Right, we're in the Ockham stack south of Heathrow. Approach control gave us a heading from Ockham that led me to believe that we were around twenty-four miles from touchdown for 28L. From our altitude of 7000ft, that was a perfect distance for us to lose the altitude easily and without any rush or too steep an angle.

We were given descent to 3000ft, told we had fifteen miles to touchdown and asked whether that was sufficient. Quick maths calculation showed we should have been at 4500ft, so no way could we descend so quickly. "No problem," said Eddie. *Whaaaat?*

(BA would probably have said no and asked for an extended routing.) And so the descent was steepened, and with the speed brake on top of the wings deployed to keep our speed under control, we fluttered down towards the runway. We were turned onto the final approach for 28L at the correct altitude after a pretty hectic descent by the crew and a *lot* of work by both the flight crew and the cabin crew. At around four miles from touchdown, we were asked whether we could switch visually to runway 28R. *Whaaaat?* "No problem", said Eddie and proceeded to do a hard right turn followed almost immediately by a hard left turn to line up with the parallel runway 28R. We landed, and just as full reverse thrust kicked in, the controller said, "Expedite next left and call ground control." Blimey, give us a second, will ya! But it was, as usual, no problem and a magnificent display of how to fly a Boeing737.

Another impressive performance from Aer Lingus could well have ended in tragedy had it not been for the professionalism of the flight crew, ATC and Aer Lingus.

This is what happened.

An Aer Lingus flight was routing to the west of Heathrow, flying from Gatwick to Dublin, when it suffered a total electrical failure. Nasty but more especially at night in complete darkness, on the flight deck as well as outside! He had about fifteen minutes to get on the ground before the battery power and his torch power ran out. Luckily Heathrow was landing on 10L, which meant he could land fairly quickly, which he did at around 2130. Heathrow had, at the time, a night jet ban between the hours of 2330 and 0600, so it looked as if the passengers and crew would have to be put up for the night as the aircraft was not able to be repaired in time. Would you believe it? The airline scrambled a replacement aeroplane and crew, flew it from Dublin to Heathrow, loaded the passengers and their baggage and got going for Dublin before the jet ban started. Impressive, to say the least. No problem, as usual! Aer Lingus – just get it done.

# Epilogue

I hope you've enjoyed this little book of mine. All the stories are real and true. They are part of my personal collection of flight deck experiences and air traffic control situations gathered over a forty-year career in aviation. A few bits have been supplied by my colleagues, to whom I offer my thanks.

When I first joined ATC in 1973, it felt as if I'd become a member of an exclusive club, such was the camaraderie in this small, select group. There are only around 2000 Air Traffic Controllers in the UK, and I was one of them. The culture has subtly changed over the years, and towards the end of my career, it had morphed from one of relaxed professionalism and pride in what we were doing and the way we were doing it to one of "Gizz a job!" Many trainees I came across were only interested in two things – passing an exam and the money! I, on the other hand, wished to learn as much about aeroplanes and aviation as I possibly could and have as much fun as possible doing it.

Air Traffic Controllers of the future will become simply systems monitors. Humans are not good at monitoring – it becomes boring very quickly. The joy of actually throwing aeroplanes around the sky for a living looks to be part of the past.

I am eternally grateful for the career I had. My sincere thanks to everyone I've met in control rooms and flight decks. It has been a privilege.

John Campbell

March 2022

# Glossary

Aviation is full of abbreviations and codes. I'm sure I've used quite a lot in this book, so to avoid your having to search through numerous journals and magazines to discover what on earth it is I'm talking about, here are the codes you need.

**ADD** – Aircraft deferred defect. If an item on the MEL is not working but it has an ADD, the aircraft can depart to the next destination only, so long as the defect can be rectified there. If not, the aircraft cannot depart.

**APU** – Auxiliary power unit. Fitted to airliners to run various systems when the main engines are not running, for example, to cool or warm the aeroplane when it's parked at the terminal. It's mounted in the tail just under the fin, and its exhaust is usually clearly visible.

**Anaprop** – Anomalous propagation. This includes different forms of radio propagation due to an unusual distribution of temperature and humidity with height in the atmosphere. While this includes propagation with larger losses than in a standard atmosphere, in practical applications it most often refers to cases when a signal propagates beyond the normal radio horizon, which is why I could see Jersey on Bournemouth's radar and heard Frankfurt at Heathrow tower. Anaprop can also be seen on a primary radar screen as blips or blobs that are not associated with an aircraft. They can track across the screen and disappear just as quickly as they appear.

**ATCO/SATCO** – Air Traffic Control Officer/Senior Air traffic Control Officer. SATCOs are normally involved in management in some way and rarely, if ever, actually control aeroplanes.

**Backtrack** – when an aircraft taxies along the runway-in-use in the opposite direction to its take-off or landing direction.

**BEA** – British European Airways. Merged with BOAC (British Overseas Airways Corporation) to become British Airways.

**CofA** – Certificate of Airworthiness. All aircraft need this before they are allowed to fly.

**CTZ** – Control Zone. Established around major airports to protect their traffic from other aircraft. Most require permission from ATC to enter.

**Echelon** – the pattern in a formation. Echelon Starboard – you are flying to the right of the lead aircraft to avoid the turbulence created. Echelon Port is the opposite – you are to the left of the lead aeroplane. Canada Geese are extremely proficient at flying in echelon.

**FL** – Flight level. Aircraft altimeters measure the distance above a given pressure datum. There are three types of pressure data used in aviation:

QFE is the air pressure at aerodrome level, so the altimeter will read zero when the aeroplane is on the ground at the airport. When flying using the QFE, the altimeter indicates height.

QNH is the air pressure at sea level. Therefore, when the aeroplane is on the ground using the QNH, the altimeter will indicate the airport's elevation (how high it is above sea level). When the aircraft is flying on the QNH, the altimeter indicates the aircraft's altitude.

When aircraft are flying between airports where the pressure can be different from each other, they will fly using the same pressure setting so that ATC can keep them 1000ft apart vertically. These are called flight levels.

To keep it simple, if we're flying towards the east, we'll be flying at an odd-numbered FL and even-numbered when flying west.

**Fam Flight** – Familiarisation flight. These were offered to and were expected to be accepted by ATCOs. Twice a year, we would join the flight crew on a return flight from our local airport. Designed to increase each other's knowledge of what we were all trying to achieve, they were most enjoyable and taught me a great deal about the workload involved in flying an airliner at any particular section of the flight.

**FAT** – Final Approach Track. This is the last leg in an aircraft's approach to the airport when the aircraft is lined up with the runway and descending for the landing.

**GMC** – Ground movement control of aircraft and vehicles at busy airports.

**Magenta line** – first observed in the Boeing 757. This line is on a screen directly in front of the pilot and displays exactly where the aeroplane is, where it has been and where it's going, all done automatically. The magenta colour was chosen because it's easy to see, especially in bright sunlight.

**MEL**- Minimum Equipment List. This is a list which provides for the operation of an aircraft with particular equipment inoperable, subject to specified conditions.

**NDB** – Non-directional beacon. This is a radio transmitter at a known location used as an aviation navigational aid. As the name implies, the signal transmitted does not include directional information. NDB signals follow the curvature of the Earth, so they can be received at substantial distances, especially at lower altitudes.

However, NDB signals are also affected by atmospheric conditions, mountainous terrain, coastal refraction and electrical storms, particularly at long range, so are mostly used as locator beacons for airports.

**No2 Director** – Most airports have an approach control wherein live the radar screens. At busy airports, there can be more than one ATCO controlling the traffic in Approach Control. The No1 controller marshals the aircraft into a rough order of landing and hands them over to the No2, who positions them onto the final approach of the runway six miles apart (two-and-a-half at Heathrow!) and at speeds which avoid the followers catching the traffic ahead. It takes much concentration to achieve this, and if it's done correctly and carefully, it keeps the traffic moving efficiently and cuts down delays.

**Procedural control** – a form of air traffic control that can be provided to aircraft in regions or airports without radar. This is done by providing horizontal separation between aircraft based on time, the geography of predetermined routes, or aircraft position reports based on ground-based navigation aids for those aircraft that are not vertically separated.

**Reaction controls** – The reaction control system on Harrier aircraft uses thrusters at the aircraft extremities (nose, tail and wingtips). Thrust from the engine can be temporarily syphoned to control the aircraft's pitch, roll and yaw before it is going fast enough for the elevators, rudder and ailerons to become effective.

**RAT** – Ram air turbine. This is a small wind turbine fitted to most military aircraft that is connected to a hydraulic pump or electrical generator and used as a power source should the engine fail. It drops down into the airflow that drives the turbine.

**SSR** – Secondary surveillance radar is a radar system used in air traffic control that, unlike primary radar systems that measure the bearing and distance of targets using the detected reflections of radio signals, relies on targets equipped with a radar transponder that reply to each interrogation signal by the radar antenna.

**TCAS** – Traffic collision avoidance system.

**VOR** – VHF Omni-Range. In radio navigation, a VOR/DME is a radio beacon that combines a VHF omnidirectional range (VOR) with a distance-measuring instrument (DME). The VOR allows the receiver to measure its bearing to or from the beacon, while the DME provides the slant distance between the receiver and the station. A VOR is much more accurate than an NDB.

# Phonetic alphabet

A Alpha .......................................N November

B Bravo .......................................O Oscar

C Charlie ....................................P Papa

D Delta .......................................Q Quebec

E Echo .........................................R Romeo

F Foxtrot ....................................S Sierra

G Golf .........................................T Tango

H Hotel .......................................U Uniform

I India .........................................V Victor

J Juliet ........................................W Whiskey

K Kilo ..........................................X Xray

L Lima .........................................Y Yankee

M Mike ........................................Z Zulu

Ingram Content Group UK Ltd.
Milton Keynes UK
UKHW020047190523
421973UK00011B/167